Chapter 1: Introduction

Welcome to the exciting journey of planning your dream wedding! As you embark on this adventure, it's essential to recognize that this chapter is not just an introduction to a book; it's the gateway to a transformative experience. "Empowered Bride" is not merely about checklists and timelines; it's about empowering you to embrace self-care throughout your wedding planning process.

Wedding planning is a beautiful and significant life event, but it comes with its fair share of challenges. It's easy to get caught up in the whirlwind of decisions, from choosing the perfect venue to finalizing the guest list. Amidst the excitement, it's crucial to remember that the most important person in this entire process is you.

In this chapter, we lay the foundation for a journey that goes beyond the logistical details of your wedding. We delve into the profound significance of self-care and set the tone for a joyous and balanced experience. Planning a wedding is not just about creating a memorable day; it's about creating a memorable season in your life.

We start by emphasizing the importance of self-care during this unique time. It's not a luxury; it's a necessity. By understanding and acknowledging the need for self-care, you are taking the first step towards ensuring that your wedding planning journey is as fulfilling and enjoyable as the big day itself.

Setting realistic expectations is another key aspect we explore. It's easy to be swept away by Pinterest-perfect images and societal expectations, but we encourage you to set your own standards and embrace the journey at your pace. This chapter aims to guide you in creating a positive mindset, one that will serve as the cornerstone of your entire wedding experience.

So, dear bride-to-be, welcome to "Empowered Bride." Get ready to not only plan a beautiful wedding but also to embark on a transformative and self-affirming journey that will leave you feeling empowered, radiant, and ready for the wedding of your dreams.

The Importance of Self-Care During Wedding Planning

Congratulations on your engagement! As you step into the whirlwind of wedding planning, it's easy to become consumed by the details, the deadlines, and the seemingly endless to-do lists. In the midst of all this excitement, it's crucial to pause and recognize the importance of self-care during this transformative period of your life.

Wedding planning is a unique and joyous experience, but it can also be overwhelming. From choosing the perfect dress to deciding on the ideal floral arrangements, the decisions can seem endless. In the midst of all the planning, it's easy to neglect the most critical component of this entire process—you.

Self-care isn't a luxury; it's a necessity, especially during the whirlwind of wedding planning. It's more than just a pampering session or a spa day; it's about intentionally taking care of your physical, emotional, and mental well-being. Think of it as giving yourself the love and attention you deserve, much like you're pouring into the wedding preparations.

The journey toward a wedding day is often described as a rollercoaster of emotions, and rightfully so. There's the joy of finding the perfect venue, the stress of managing the budget, the excitement of saying yes to the dress, and the occasional moments of anxiety as the big day approaches. With all these emotions in play, it becomes paramount to establish a self-care routine that acts as your anchor, keeping you grounded and centered throughout the process.

One of the key reasons self-care is vital during wedding planning is its positive impact on stress management. Planning a wedding can be stressful, no matter how organized and well-prepared you are. Stress is a natural part of the process, but how you manage it makes all the difference. Incorporating self-care practices into your routine can significantly reduce stress levels, allowing you to approach each task with a clearer mind and a more positive outlook.

Moreover, self-care enhances your overall well-being, both physically and mentally. Adequate sleep, regular exercise, and healthy eating habits contribute to increased energy levels, improved mood, and enhanced focus. As you navigate the intricacies of wedding planning, having a well-nourished and well-rested body and mind will undoubtedly contribute to a more enjoyable experience.

Beyond the physical aspects, self-care plays a crucial role in emotional well-being. Wedding planning often involves navigating complex family dynamics, making tough decisions, and managing expectations. Taking time for self-reflection, setting boundaries, and seeking support when needed are all part of the emotional self-care journey. It's about honoring your feelings, acknowledging the challenges, and celebrating the victories, no matter how small.

In essence, the importance of self-care during wedding planning lies in its ability to ensure that you, the radiant bride, are not only creating a beautiful celebration but also nurturing your own well-being. Remember, your wedding day is a reflection of your love story, and that story begins with how you care for yourself during this exciting chapter. So, amidst the floral arrangements and seating charts, don't forget to prioritize the most important person in this journey—you.

Setting Realistic Expectations for the Journey

Welcome to the wonderful world of wedding planning! As you embark on this exhilarating journey, it's crucial to set the stage with a healthy dose of realistic expectations. While Pinterest boards and romantic movies may paint a picture of flawless weddings, the reality is that planning such a significant event comes with its share of challenges and surprises.

Setting realistic expectations doesn't mean dulling the sparkle of your dreams; instead, it's about approaching the process with a clear understanding of what to anticipate. Think of it as creating a roadmap that acknowledges both the breathtaking highs and the occasional bumps in the road.

To begin, let's talk timelines. While we'd all love to have an unlimited timeframe to plan the perfect wedding, the reality is often different. Many couples find themselves navigating the delicate balance of work, social commitments, and, of course, their personal lives. Setting realistic expectations in terms of time involves recognizing that some aspects of planning will require more time and attention than others. Be prepared for a few time-consuming tasks, and don't be too hard on yourself if the journey takes a bit longer than expected.

Budgeting is another area where realistic expectations play a pivotal role. Weddings can be expensive, and while it's wonderful to dream big, it's equally important to establish a budget that aligns with your financial reality. Setting realistic financial expectations involves open communication with your partner about your priorities and non-negotiables. It's about finding a balance between creating a magical day and ensuring you start your married life on solid financial ground.

Now, let's talk about decision-making. From the color of the flowers to the flavor of the cake, wedding planning involves countless decisions, both big and small. Setting realistic expectations in this realm means understanding that not every decision will come effortlessly. There may be moments of indecision or even a change of heart. Embrace the process, and remember that it's perfectly normal for your vision to evolve as you move forward.

Family dynamics and expectations are also factors to consider when setting realistic expectations. Navigating the expectations of both your and your partner's families can be a delicate dance. Recognize that not everyone will have the same vision for the wedding, and compromises may be necessary. Open and honest communication, coupled with a realistic understanding of differing perspectives, will be your best allies in these situations.

Lastly, setting realistic expectations involves acknowledging that perfection is a myth. No wedding is flawless, and that's part of what makes each celebration unique and memorable. Unexpected challenges may arise, but it's your attitude and resilience that will make the difference. Embrace the imperfections as part of your story, and remember that the true magic lies in the love you're celebrating.

In conclusion, setting realistic expectations for the wedding planning journey is not about lowering your standards; it's about approaching the process with a clear-eyed perspective. By doing so, you empower yourself to navigate the twists and turns with grace, allowing the true beauty of your love story to shine through every step of the way. So, let the journey begin with a heart full of excitement, a mind grounded in reality, and the knowledge that your wedding will be a reflection of your unique and beautiful story.

Creating a Positive Mindset for a Joyful Wedding Experience

Congratulations on taking the plunge into wedding planning! As you embark on this exhilarating adventure, one of the most valuable tools you can carry with you is a positive mindset. While the road to your dream wedding may have a few twists and turns, cultivating positivity will not only enhance your overall experience but also contribute to a truly joyful celebration.

Let's start with the power of perspective. Wedding planning, much like any significant endeavor, is all about how you choose to view it. Instead of getting bogged down by the details or overwhelmed by the seemingly endless decisions, consider framing each task as a step closer to creating a day that reflects your unique love story. Embrace the process, and remember that each decision, no matter how small, is a building block for your dream wedding.

Positivity also plays a crucial role in managing stress. The reality is that there will be moments of stress during wedding planning—whether it's dealing with budget concerns, family dynamics, or unexpected hiccups. However, by maintaining a positive mindset, you equip yourself with the resilience to navigate these challenges. Rather than viewing stress as a hindrance, see it as an opportunity for growth and problem-solving. You'll find that challenges are not roadblocks but rather stepping stones to a more robust and resilient relationship.

Moreover, a positive mindset influences the energy you bring into the planning process. Enthusiasm and optimism are contagious, and by radiating positivity, you create an uplifting atmosphere for everyone involved. Your excitement will not only inspire those around you but will also infuse joy into every aspect of the wedding preparations. Remember, the journey should be as memorable as the destination, and a positive mindset ensures that the memories created along the way are filled with laughter and love.

Another aspect to consider is the impact of positivity on decision-making. A positive mindset allows you to approach choices with clarity and confidence. Instead of getting bogged down by doubts or second-guessing, focus on the excitement of making decisions that align with your vision. Trust your instincts, and remember that there's no one right way to plan a wedding. Your positive mindset will guide you toward choices that resonate with your unique style and preferences.

Lastly, cultivating a positive mindset involves practicing gratitude. Take a moment each day to reflect on the aspects of wedding planning that bring you joy and appreciation. Whether it's the support of loved ones, the thrill of finding the perfect venue, or the anticipation of exchanging vows, acknowledging the positive elements in your journey will create a ripple effect of gratitude and joy.

In conclusion, creating a positive mindset for your wedding experience is not just about wishful thinking; it's a powerful tool that shapes the entire journey. Approach each day with a heart full of optimism, a mind focused on solutions, and an awareness of the joy woven into every decision. By doing so, you not only ensure a more enjoyable wedding planning process but also set the stage for a celebration that radiates with the positivity and love that define your relationship. So, with a smile on your face and excitement in your heart, let the journey to your dream wedding begin!

Chapter 2: Understanding Your Needs

Welcome to Chapter 2 of your wedding planning journey, where we delve into the heart of what makes this experience uniquely yours—Understanding Your Needs. As you embark on this adventure, it's essential to take a moment to turn the spotlight inward and recognize the intricacies of your desires, priorities, and well-being.

This chapter is not just about logistics; it's about the beautiful tapestry of your personality, values, and dreams that will weave through every aspect of your wedding celebration. Your needs are the compass that will guide you through the myriad decisions, and understanding them is the key to crafting a day that authentically reflects who you are.

We start by encouraging you to reflect on your personal values and priorities. Your wedding is a celebration of your love story, and understanding what matters most to you lays the foundation for a meaningful and authentic event. Whether it's creating an intimate atmosphere, incorporating cultural traditions, or prioritizing sustainability, this chapter invites you to embrace what resonates deeply with your heart.

Next, we explore the art of identifying stress triggers and coping mechanisms. Wedding planning, as exciting as it is, can be a rollercoaster of emotions. By recognizing the factors that may cause stress and implementing effective coping strategies, you empower yourself to navigate challenges with resilience and grace. It's not just about planning a wedding; it's about fostering emotional well-being throughout the process.

Building a support system is another crucial aspect of understanding your needs. Friends, family, and your wedding team are all integral parts of your support network. This chapter guides you in recognizing the roles each plays in your journey, fostering open communication, and seeking the support you need. After all, a joy shared is a joy doubled, and the process of understanding your needs extends beyond the individual to the community that surrounds you.

In essence, this chapter is a celebration of you—your values, your emotions, and your connections. It's an exploration of the intricate tapestry that makes you, the radiant bride, unique. By understanding your needs, you pave the way for a wedding that not only dazzles the eyes but also touches the soul. So, take a deep breath, embrace the journey inward, and let's uncover the layers of what truly matters to you as you craft the wedding day of your dreams.

Reflecting on Personal Values and Priorities

Welcome to the heart of your wedding planning journey—reflecting on your personal values and priorities. Your wedding day is not just an event; it's a reflection of who you are, what you believe in, and the love story you're about to share with the world. In this section, we embark on a journey of self-discovery to uncover the values and priorities that will shape your wedding into a truly authentic and meaningful celebration.

Begin by taking a moment to reflect on your core values. These are the guiding principles that define you as an individual and as a couple. Consider what matters most to you in life—whether it's family, community, adventure, or creativity. Identifying these values lays the foundation for a wedding that aligns with your deepest beliefs and resonates with authenticity.

As you reflect on your values, think about how they can be woven into the fabric of your wedding day. For example, if family is a central value, you might explore ways to incorporate family traditions, involve loved ones in the planning process, or create a ceremony that celebrates the unity of two families coming together. Your values are the brushstrokes that paint the canvas of your wedding, infusing it with personal significance and depth.

Next, consider your priorities for the wedding day. What aspects of the celebration are most important to you? Whether it's the venue, the ceremony, the food, or the overall atmosphere, identifying your priorities allows you to allocate time, energy, and resources to the elements that matter most. This isn't about conforming to societal expectations; it's about creating a day that reflects your unique vision and brings you the greatest joy.

Explore your creative side by brainstorming ways to infuse your values and priorities into different aspects of the wedding. If environmental sustainability is a priority, you might opt for eco-friendly decor, locally sourced catering, or even a green venue. The beauty of reflecting on values and priorities is that it opens up a world of creative possibilities, allowing you to design a wedding day that feels not only beautiful but also deeply meaningful.

Moreover, this reflection process is an opportunity for you and your partner to align your values and priorities. Discuss openly and honestly, sharing your thoughts and listening to your partner's perspectives. Finding common ground ensures that your wedding is a joint expression of your shared values and a celebration of the unique qualities each of you brings to the relationship.

In essence, reflecting on your personal values and priorities is the cornerstone of a wedding that goes beyond the surface. It's about infusing your celebration with the essence of who you are and what you hold dear. So, grab a notebook, sit down with your partner, and let the exploration begin. The journey of self-discovery is not only a vital part of wedding planning; it's a beautiful process that sets the stage for a day that is authentically and undeniably yours.

Identifying Stress Triggers and Coping Mechanisms

Let's dive into a crucial aspect of your wedding planning journey—identifying stress triggers and discovering effective coping mechanisms. Planning a wedding is undoubtedly a joyous adventure, but it's not without its share of challenges and, yes, moments of stress. This section is all about equipping yourself with the self-awareness and tools to navigate those stressors with resilience and grace.

Begin by taking a reflective pause. Consider the aspects of wedding planning that have the potential to trigger stress. It might be the pressure of making decisions, the demands of coordinating with vendors, or even the expectations from family and friends. Acknowledging these stress triggers is the first step toward understanding how to manage them effectively.

Once you've identified your stress triggers, it's time to explore coping mechanisms that work for you. Coping mechanisms are like a personalized toolkit that you can turn to when the going gets tough. They can vary from person to person, so it's essential to discover what resonates with you. Some people find solace in physical activities like exercise or yoga, while others may turn to creative outlets like journaling or art.

Consider what has helped you cope with stress in the past and experiment with new techniques. Whether it's taking a leisurely walk, practicing deep breathing exercises, or indulging in a favorite hobby, finding healthy coping mechanisms ensures that you have a reliable set of tools to turn to when stress makes an appearance.

Open communication with your partner is also crucial during this process. Share your stress triggers and coping mechanisms with each other, fostering an environment of mutual support. Knowing that you have someone by your side who understands your sources of stress and can offer encouragement is invaluable. This shared understanding strengthens your connection and makes the wedding planning journey a collaborative effort.

In addition to individual coping mechanisms, consider incorporating joint stress-relief activities into your routine. This could be anything from a weekly date night to a weekend getaway. By consciously setting aside time to relax and recharge together, you reinforce the idea that wedding planning is not just about the destination but also about the journey you embark on as a couple.

Furthermore, don't forget the power of perspective. It's easy to get caught up in the minutiae of wedding details, but taking a step back and reminding yourself of the bigger picture can be incredibly grounding. Consider creating a mantra or affirmation that resonates with you and reflects your values. When stress creeps in, repeating this mantra can serve as a powerful reminder of what truly matters.

In conclusion, identifying stress triggers and uncovering effective coping mechanisms is a proactive and empowering approach to wedding planning. It's about understanding yourself, recognizing potential challenges, and equipping yourself with the tools to overcome them. As you navigate this transformative journey, remember that stress is a natural part of the process, but with self-awareness and positive coping strategies, you're well-prepared to embrace the adventure with resilience and joy.

Building a Support System: Friends, Family, and Wedding Team

As you embark on the exciting journey of planning your wedding, you'll quickly discover the immense value of having a robust support system in place. Your support network, comprised of friends, family, and your dedicated wedding team, plays a pivotal role in ensuring that the entire process is not just manageable but also filled with joy and shared moments.

Let's start with friends—the ones who have been by your side through thick and thin. Share your excitement and concerns with them. Whether it's a casual chat over coffee or a dedicated wedding planning session, friends bring a unique perspective and often serve as a sounding board for your ideas. Their encouragement and honest feedback can be invaluable as you navigate the myriad decisions that come with planning a wedding.

Family, too, is a cornerstone of your support system. While family dynamics can sometimes add complexity to the planning process, open communication is key. Clearly express your expectations and listen to theirs. Engage family members in specific aspects of the planning that align with their strengths and interests. When everyone is on the same page, the planning journey becomes a collaborative effort, strengthening familial bonds and creating cherished memories along the way.

Your wedding team, consisting of vendors, planners, and anyone else helping to bring your vision to life, is a crucial component of your support network. Choose professionals who not only understand your vision but also make you feel at ease. Communication is paramount here as well—clearly articulate your expectations and listen to their expertise. A harmonious relationship with your wedding team ensures that you can trust them to execute your vision, allowing you to focus on enjoying the journey.

Open and honest communication is a common thread that ties together all aspects of your support system. Clearly expressing your needs, sharing your concerns, and celebrating victories foster a sense of community around your wedding planning. It's about building a network that not only supports you practically but also emotionally.

Remember, your support system is there not just for the logistics but also for the emotional aspects of the journey. When the stress levels rise, having loved ones to lean on can make all the difference. Whether it's a reassuring word from a friend, a comforting hug from a family member, or the expertise of a trusted vendor, your support system provides a safety net that allows you to navigate challenges with confidence.

Furthermore, involving your support system in the celebration itself adds an extra layer of significance to your wedding. Whether it's having a close friend as your maid of honor, a family member perform a special reading during the ceremony, or your wedding team going above and beyond to create a memorable experience, the shared involvement of your support network enriches the entire celebration.

In conclusion, building a robust support system is not just a practical consideration; it's a conscious choice to surround yourself with positivity, understanding, and shared joy. Your friends, family, and wedding team are not just participants in the wedding; they are active contributors to the narrative of your love story. As you navigate the intricate details of planning, let your support system be the wind beneath your wings, lifting you up and ensuring that the journey is as magical as the destination.

Chapter 3: Establishing a Wellness Routine

Welcome to Chapter 3 of your wedding planning journey, where we shift our focus from the external elements of the celebration to the internal—you. "Establishing a Wellness Routine" is not just a chapter; it's a guide to nurturing your well-being as you navigate the beautiful chaos of wedding preparations.

Your well-being is at the heart of this chapter, and we're here to explore how establishing a wellness routine can transform your wedding planning experience. Planning a wedding is a remarkable journey, but it can also be demanding. This chapter invites you to prioritize self-care, not as an indulgence but as a fundamental aspect of creating a wedding that reflects your joy, radiance, and, most importantly, a balanced and healthy version of you.

We'll delve into the physical, mental, and emotional aspects of wellness, recognizing that a holistic approach is key to ensuring you feel your best on the big day. From incorporating exercise into your routine to exploring mindfulness practices for stress reduction, we'll guide you in crafting a wellness routine that aligns with your unique needs and preferences.

The journey toward a radiant and joyful wedding involves more than just ticking off items on a checklist. It's about embracing a lifestyle that nourishes your mind, body, and spirit. As you engage in the various elements of this chapter, remember that wellness is not a destination but a continuous journey—one that begins now and extends far beyond the wedding day.

So, grab a cup of tea, find a comfortable spot, and let's explore the world of wellness together. This chapter is an invitation to prioritize yourself, to savor the journey, and to infuse every moment with the positive energy that comes from caring for your well-being. Here's to a wellness routine that not only enhances your wedding planning experience but also lays the foundation for a lifetime of radiant moments. Let the journey within begin!

Incorporating Physical Exercise into a Busy Schedule

As you navigate the myriad tasks and decisions that come with planning your dream wedding, it's easy to let physical exercise fall to the wayside. However, incorporating regular exercise into your busy schedule is not just about fitting into that perfect wedding dress or looking fantastic in photos—it's a key component of maintaining your overall well-being during this exhilarating yet demanding time.

Let's acknowledge the reality of a busy schedule. With appointments, meetings, vendor discussions, and an ever-growing to-do list, finding time for physical activity might seem like an impossible feat. The key is to view exercise not as an additional task but as an essential investment in your health and mental well-being.

Start by reframing your perspective on exercise. It's not just a chore; it's a gift you give yourself. Physical activity releases endorphins, those feel-good hormones that can help alleviate stress and boost your mood. This positive energy isn't just beneficial for your well-being; it can significantly impact how you approach and handle the challenges of wedding planning.

Consider the practicality of your schedule and identify windows of opportunity for exercise. Whether it's a brisk morning walk, a quick home workout, or a dance session in the living room, find activities that seamlessly fit into your routine. This isn't about carving out hours at the gym; it's about making the most of the time you have.

Involve your partner in the process. Not only does exercising together provide quality time, but it also creates a support system for mutual motivation. Whether you opt for a joint workout session or simply encourage each other to stay active, having a fitness buddy can make the experience more enjoyable and sustainable.

Explore activities that align with your interests. If the thought of a traditional gym session doesn't excite you, consider alternative forms of exercise that bring joy. Whether it's hiking, dancing, yoga, or even trying a new sport together, the key is to find activities that you genuinely enjoy. This way, exercise becomes a pleasurable break from the wedding planning hustle rather than an additional stressor.

Embrace the power of consistency over intensity. Instead of setting lofty fitness goals that may be challenging to maintain, focus on establishing a consistent routine. Short, frequent sessions can be just as effective as longer workouts, and they're often more feasible within a busy schedule.

Remember that every bit of movement counts. Whether it's taking the stairs instead of the elevator, doing quick stretches during breaks, or incorporating physical activity into daily tasks, these small efforts add up over time. The goal is not perfection but progress— a commitment to prioritizing your well-being in the midst of wedding planning.

In conclusion, incorporating physical exercise into a busy schedule is a deliberate choice to invest in yourself. It's not just about the physical benefits; it's a holistic approach to maintaining your mental and emotional well-being during this transformative period. As you embrace the joy and excitement of wedding planning, let physical activity be a source of positive energy, resilience, and a reminder that taking care of yourself is an essential part of the journey.

Mindfulness Practices for Stress Reduction

In the whirlwind of wedding planning, moments of stress can become a familiar companion. That's where mindfulness practices come in—your allies in creating a sense of calm and grounding amidst the bustling excitement. Mindfulness is more than just a trendy buzzword; it's a powerful tool that can help you navigate stress, stay present, and approach each aspect of planning with a clear and focused mind.

Let's start by understanding what mindfulness truly means. At its core, mindfulness is about being fully present in the current moment without judgment. It's about embracing the here and now, acknowledging your thoughts and feelings without getting entangled in them. In the context of wedding planning, mindfulness provides a sanctuary of calm within the storm.

One of the simplest and most accessible mindfulness practices is conscious breathing. When stress starts to build, take a moment to pause and focus on your breath. Inhale deeply, feeling the air fill your lungs, and then exhale slowly, releasing any tension. This intentional breathwork has a profound impact on your nervous system, signaling to your body that it's okay to relax.

Mindful walking is another practice that seamlessly integrates into your daily routine. Whether you're strolling through a park, walking to a meeting, or simply moving around your home, bring your attention to each step. Feel the connection between your feet and the ground, notice the sensations in your body, and allow your mind to settle into the rhythm of your movement. It's a gentle reminder that even in motion, you can find moments of stillness.

Body scan meditation is a mindfulness practice that encourages you to direct your attention to different parts of your body, noting any sensations without judgment. This practice is particularly effective for releasing tension and bringing awareness to areas where stress may manifest physically. As you navigate the intricate details of wedding planning, a body scan can be a quick and effective reset button.

Cultivating mindfulness doesn't always require formal meditation. Everyday activities can become opportunities for mindfulness when approached with intention. Whether you're savoring a cup of tea, enjoying a meal, or even washing dishes, immerse yourself fully in the experience. Engage your senses, notice the details, and let go of distractions. These small moments of mindfulness can act as anchors throughout your day.

Incorporating mindfulness into your routine is not about adding another task to your to-do list. It's about infusing awareness into what you're already doing. Before diving into a wedding planning session, take a few moments to center yourself. Close your eyes, take a few deep breaths, and set an intention for the task ahead. This simple ritual creates a bridge between the external demands and your internal sense of calm.

As you explore mindfulness practices for stress reduction, remember that it's a journey, not a destination. Be patient with yourself, embrace imperfections, and celebrate the moments of peace you cultivate along the way. Mindfulness is a gift you give yourself, a sanctuary of stillness that exists within you, ready to be accessed whenever the whirlwind of wedding planning starts to swirl.

The Importance of Adequate Sleep and Restorative Rest

In the midst of the excitement and activity that accompanies wedding planning, the importance of adequate sleep and restorative rest can often be overlooked. Yet, these elements are fundamental to your overall well-being, affecting not only your physical health but also your mental and emotional resilience. Let's explore why a good night's sleep and intentional rest are essential components of your self-care routine during this transformative time.

First and foremost, sleep is a cornerstone of your body's ability to function optimally. It's during sleep that your body undergoes crucial processes like tissue repair, muscle growth, and the release of hormones that regulate growth and stress. In essence, a good night's sleep is like a reset button for your body, allowing it to recover and prepare for the demands of the day ahead.

Consider the impact of sleep on your mental and emotional well-being. A well-rested mind is more alert, focused, and better equipped to handle the myriad decisions and tasks associated with wedding planning. On the flip side, inadequate sleep can contribute to stress, mood swings, and difficulty concentrating. By prioritizing sleep, you're not just investing in physical health; you're nurturing your mental and emotional resilience.

In the context of wedding planning, where emotions can run high and the to-do list seems never-ending, quality sleep becomes a non-negotiable ally. Establishing a consistent sleep routine, with a focus on creating a calming bedtime environment, can significantly improve both the duration and quality of your sleep. This routine might include winding down with a book, minimizing screen time before bed, or practicing relaxation techniques.

Restorative rest goes beyond nightly sleep; it involves intentional moments of rejuvenation throughout your day. Consider incorporating short breaks into your schedule to recharge your energy and clear your mind. Whether it's a brief walk, a few minutes of deep breathing, or a moment of quiet reflection, these pauses contribute to overall well-being and can enhance your productivity and focus.

Moreover, the concept of "rest" extends beyond physical rejuvenation to include emotional and mental rest. Wedding planning can be emotionally taxing, and giving yourself permission to step away from the planning process, even briefly, is crucial. It's about acknowledging your feelings, setting boundaries, and creating space for activities that bring you joy and relaxation.

As you navigate the demands of wedding planning, it's tempting to sacrifice sleep and rest in the name of productivity. However, the irony is that adequate rest enhances your efficiency and effectiveness in the long run. It's a foundational element that supports your ability to make thoughtful decisions, maintain a positive mindset, and approach challenges with resilience.

In conclusion, the importance of adequate sleep and restorative rest cannot be overstated. As you embark on this transformative journey of wedding planning, view sleep and intentional rest as non-negotiable components of your self-care routine. They are not indulgences but rather essential elements that contribute to your overall well-being. By prioritizing rest, you're not just preparing for the wedding day; you're nurturing the best version of yourself, ready to embrace each moment of the journey with vitality and grace.

Chapter 4: Navigating Emotional Challenges

Welcome to Chapter 4 of your wedding planning adventure—Navigating Emotional Challenges. As you immerse yourself in the intricate details of creating a day that reflects your love story, it's inevitable that you'll encounter a spectrum of emotions. This chapter is your guide through the emotional landscape of wedding planning, offering insights, strategies, and a reassuring reminder that you're not alone in experiencing the highs and lows of this transformative journey.

Wedding planning is a unique emotional rollercoaster. From the exhilaration of saying "Yes" to the dress to the occasional challenges of managing differing opinions and expectations, your emotional landscape is as much a part of the journey as the tangible elements of the celebration. This chapter invites you to embrace the full spectrum of emotions, recognizing them as integral threads in the tapestry of your love story.

We'll start by acknowledging the joyous moments—the excitement of envisioning your dream ceremony, the thrill of selecting the perfect venue, and the warmth that comes with each supportive gesture from friends and family. These are the moments that make wedding planning a celebration in itself, a journey filled with anticipation and love.

However, it's equally important to navigate the more challenging emotions that may arise. Whether it's the pressure of making decisions, the stress of managing a budget, or the inevitable moments of tension with loved ones, this chapter provides insights into understanding, processing, and effectively managing these emotional challenges. We'll explore communication strategies, coping mechanisms, and the art of finding balance amidst the complexities.

Your emotional well-being is at the forefront of this chapter, recognizing that a positive and resilient mindset is key to savoring the joyous moments and gracefully navigating the challenges. As you delve into the pages ahead, remember that the emotions you experience are not just part of the process—they are reflections of the depth and significance of the commitment you're making.

So, let's embark on this emotional journey together. Whether you're riding the highs of excitement or facing the lows of stress, know that each emotion is a brushstroke on the canvas of your love story. Embrace the journey, cherish the moments, and trust that, at the end of this adventure, the tapestry woven will be a beautiful reflection of the love that binds you and your partner. Let the exploration of emotional challenges begin!

Managing Relationship Dynamics During Wedding Planning

Navigating the intricate terrain of wedding planning often brings to light the importance of managing relationship dynamics. As you and your partner embark on this transformative journey, it's not uncommon to encounter varying opinions, expectations, and perhaps the occasional disagreement. This section is dedicated to providing insights and strategies for fostering open communication, understanding, and harmony as you navigate the beautiful complexities of planning your special day together.

First and foremost, recognize that wedding planning involves a blend of individual dreams and shared visions. Your partner may have different preferences, priorities, or ideas about certain aspects of the celebration. The key is to approach these differences with an open heart and a willingness to understand each other's perspectives.

Communication is the linchpin of managing relationship dynamics during wedding planning. Create a safe space for open and honest conversations about your expectations, desires, and concerns. Establishing effective communication early on sets the tone for collaborative decision-making and ensures that both partners feel heard and valued.

Set aside dedicated time for wedding planning discussions, creating an environment free from distractions where you can focus on the task at hand. Use this time not only to discuss practical details but also to check in with each other emotionally. Ask about your partner's feelings, listen actively, and validate their perspective. This practice not only enhances your planning efficiency but also strengthens your emotional connection.

Embrace compromise as a cornerstone of managing relationship dynamics. Recognize that each decision is an opportunity to find middle ground, blending elements of both your visions to create a celebration that reflects your unique partnership. Compromise is not about sacrifice; it's about finding creative solutions that honor both individuals in the relationship.

It's essential to maintain perspective and prioritize what truly matters. In the grand scheme of your relationship, the color of the flowers or the choice of music may seem insignificant compared to the commitment you're making to each other. Keeping this perspective allows you to approach decisions with a sense of levity and prevents minor disagreements from overshadowing the joyous nature of the occasion.

In the face of potential disagreements, practice active listening and empathy. Seek to understand your partner's point of view before expressing your own. This not only fosters a sense of mutual respect but also creates an atmosphere where both partners feel comfortable sharing their thoughts and concerns. Remember, you're a team, and tackling challenges together strengthens your bond.

If you find that certain aspects of wedding planning are causing tension, consider enlisting the help of a neutral third party, such as a wedding planner or a trusted friend. Having an external perspective can provide valuable insights and facilitate compromise, ensuring that the planning process remains a positive and collaborative experience.

Lastly, celebrate the victories together, both big and small. Acknowledge the progress you make in planning, savor the joyful moments, and express gratitude for the shared effort. By recognizing and celebrating each other's contributions, you reinforce the idea that, ultimately, the wedding is a celebration of your partnership—a journey that you're navigating together with love, understanding, and a shared vision for the future.

Dealing with Family Expectations and Dynamics

Dealing with family expectations and dynamics is a delicate dance within the intricate choreography of wedding planning. Families, with their unique dynamics and expectations, can play a significant role in the celebration, adding warmth and support but also introducing a layer of complexity. This section is dedicated to navigating the nuances of family dynamics, fostering open communication, and finding a balance that allows everyone to contribute to the joyous occasion.

First and foremost, recognize that family members may have their own visions and expectations for the wedding. Whether it's traditions, cultural practices, or specific preferences, these elements contribute to the rich tapestry of your family's identity. Approach conversations about family expectations with respect and a genuine desire to understand the significance behind these requests.

Effective communication becomes paramount when addressing family expectations. Establish an open dialogue early in the planning process, allowing family members to share their thoughts and expectations. Create a space where everyone feels heard, and be prepared to listen actively, acknowledging the importance of each family member's perspective.

In situations where family expectations may differ from your own vision, seek common ground and explore creative solutions. Compromise becomes a valuable tool in finding resolutions that honor both your desires and your family's wishes. This doesn't mean sacrificing your vision; rather, it involves identifying areas where compromise is possible and maintaining the essence of what matters most to you.

Set clear boundaries from the outset, establishing guidelines for collaboration and communication. Clearly communicate your preferences and decisions to avoid misunderstandings later on. Boundaries also involve recognizing when to seek a balance between honoring family traditions and staying true to your unique vision for the celebration.

In cases where family dynamics introduce challenges, consider enlisting the support of a neutral third party, such as a wedding planner or mediator. A professional with experience in managing family dynamics can provide guidance, offer solutions, and ensure that the planning process remains a positive and collaborative experience for everyone involved.

Embrace the opportunity to involve family members in meaningful ways. Assign specific tasks or responsibilities that align with their strengths and interests. This not only makes them feel valued and included but also allows them to contribute to the celebration in a manner that is authentic to them.

Cultural and religious considerations may also come into play, adding additional layers to family expectations. In these instances, approach conversations with sensitivity and a genuine interest in understanding the cultural or religious significance behind certain traditions. Finding a balance that respects both familial and personal values is key to creating a wedding celebration that feels authentic and inclusive.

Remember that family dynamics, though challenging at times, are a testament to the love and connections that bind you. Approach each conversation with an open heart, seeking to build bridges and strengthen relationships. The wedding planning process, when navigated with empathy and patience, can become an opportunity for growth, understanding, and the creation of lasting memories with those who matter most. In the tapestry of your wedding celebration, family expectations and dynamics are threads that weave together to create a unique and beautiful story.

Coping with the Emotional Rollercoaster: Pre-wedding Jitters and Anxiety

The emotional rollercoaster leading up to your wedding day is entirely normal, with pre-wedding jitters and anxiety being frequent passengers on this exhilarating ride. It's essential to acknowledge that amidst the joy and anticipation, feelings of nervousness and anxiety can surface. This section is dedicated to exploring these emotions, understanding their origins, and providing coping strategies to ensure that the journey to your wedding day is not just a celebration of love but also a path of emotional well-being.

First and foremost, recognize that experiencing pre-wedding jitters is not an indication of doubt or second thoughts about your decision to get married. Rather, it's a natural response to the significance of the commitment you're making. The pressure to ensure that everything goes perfectly, coupled with the heightened expectations surrounding weddings, can contribute to a range of emotions.

Communication becomes a powerful tool in managing pre-wedding jitters. Share your feelings with your partner, friends, or a trusted family member. Expressing your concerns and receiving reassurance can be incredibly comforting. Remember that your partner is likely experiencing similar emotions, and sharing your thoughts creates a space for mutual support.

Establish realistic expectations for yourself and the wedding day. It's normal to want everything to be perfect, but perfection is a subjective and often unattainable standard. Embrace the idea that the beauty of the day lies in its authenticity and the celebration of your love, rather than in flawless execution of every detail.

Practice mindfulness and stress-reduction techniques to ground yourself in the present moment. Whether it's deep breathing exercises, meditation, or simply taking moments of quiet reflection, incorporating these practices into your routine can help manage anxiety and bring a sense of calm amidst the whirlwind of preparations.

Delegate tasks and responsibilities to trusted friends, family members, or a wedding planner. Trying to manage every detail on your own can contribute to stress and anxiety. Sharing the load not only lightens the burden but also allows others to contribute to the celebration, fostering a sense of shared joy.

Maintain a healthy balance between wedding planning and self-care. Ensure that you're dedicating time to activities that bring you joy and relaxation, whether it's reading a book, going for a walk, or spending quality time with loved ones. These moments of self-care are crucial for recharging your emotional well-being.

Consider seeking support from a mental health professional if feelings of anxiety become overwhelming. A counselor or therapist can provide coping strategies, offer a non-judgmental space to express your emotions, and help you navigate the underlying causes of pre-wedding jitters.

Lastly, keep in mind that the emotional rollercoaster is a shared experience. Connect with other couples who have gone through similar feelings during their wedding planning journey. Sharing stories and insights can provide a sense of solidarity and reassurance that you're not alone in navigating the complexities of pre-wedding emotions.

In conclusion, pre-wedding jitters and anxiety are common aspects of the journey toward your special day. Embrace these emotions with compassion and understanding, recognizing that they are part of the tapestry of the wedding planning process. By prioritizing communication, self-care, and seeking support when needed, you not only manage the emotional rollercoaster but also pave the way for a wedding day filled with authenticity, joy, and the celebration of your unique love story.

Chapter 5: Crafting a Mindful Wedding Vision

Welcome to Chapter 5, where we embark on a journey of mindfulness in crafting your wedding vision. As the heart of your celebration, your wedding vision is more than just a collection of aesthetic choices; it's a reflection of your love story, values, and the unique essence of your partnership. In this chapter, we delve into the art of intentional decision-making, encouraging you to approach each element of your wedding with mindfulness and purpose.

Crafting a mindful wedding vision is about more than just creating a visually stunning event—it's an opportunity to infuse your celebration with meaning and authenticity. Whether you're envisioning an intimate gathering or a grand affair, this chapter guides you through the process of aligning your choices with your values, ensuring that your wedding day is a true reflection of who you are as a couple.

We'll explore the concept of mindfulness in the context of wedding planning, encouraging you to be present in each decision, from choosing a venue to selecting floral arrangements. Mindful decision-making involves a deep consideration of the significance behind each choice, recognizing that the details of your celebration contribute to the narrative of your love story.

Throughout this chapter, we'll discuss practical strategies for infusing mindfulness into your wedding vision. From creating a mood board that captures the emotions you want to evoke to incorporating personal touches that hold sentimental value, the goal is to guide you in making choices that resonate with authenticity and purpose.

The mindful approach to wedding planning extends beyond the visual aspects to the experiences you create for yourselves and your guests. We'll explore ways to foster a sense of connection, joy, and mindfulness on the wedding day, ensuring that the celebration is not just an event but a meaningful journey for everyone involved.

As you immerse yourself in crafting a mindful wedding vision, remember that this is a deeply personal process. It's an opportunity to celebrate your partnership in a way that feels true to you, free from external expectations and societal pressures. Your wedding vision is a canvas waiting to be painted with the strokes of your love story, and each mindful decision you make adds layers to this beautiful masterpiece.

So, let's embark on this chapter with an open heart and a clear intention—to craft a wedding vision that goes beyond the surface, inviting you and your guests into a mindful celebration of love, connection, and the beauty of the present moment. The journey to a mindful wedding vision begins now.

Defining Your Unique Wedding Style and Theme

Defining your unique wedding style and theme is the exciting first step in bringing your mindful wedding vision to life. Your wedding is an opportunity to showcase your personality, preferences, and the shared essence of your partnership. This section guides you through the process of discovering and defining the elements that will shape the overall style and theme of your celebration.

Begin by reflecting on your personal tastes and the aesthetic that resonates with both you and your partner. Consider the environments and settings where you feel most comfortable and inspired. Are you drawn to the rustic charm of nature, the elegance of a classic ballroom, or the intimate coziness of an urban loft? Your unique style is an expression of your individual and collective tastes.

Create a mood board to visually capture the atmosphere and emotions you envision for your wedding day. This can include images, colors, textures, and any other elements that resonate with your desired aesthetic. This process not only helps you clarify your vision but also serves as a valuable reference point when making decisions about decor, attire, and other visual elements.

Consider incorporating meaningful and personal touches into your wedding style. Think about elements that hold sentimental value—perhaps a color that symbolizes an important milestone in your relationship or a motif that reflects a shared passion. These personal touches infuse your wedding style with authenticity and create a deeper connection to the celebration.

Explore various themes that align with your vision and values. Whether it's a specific era, a cultural influence, or a shared interest, a theme can provide cohesion to your wedding elements. For example, if you both love travel, a vintage travel theme could inspire decor, invitations, and even the menu, creating a cohesive and memorable experience for you and your guests.

As you define your wedding style and theme, keep in mind the practical aspects of your chosen venue. Consider how the existing architecture, decor, and ambiance complement or influence your desired aesthetic. Harmonizing your style with the venue ensures a cohesive and visually pleasing experience for everyone attending.

Don't be afraid to mix and match elements to create a style that is uniquely yours. Your wedding doesn't have to fit into a predefined category; it can be a beautiful fusion of different styles that reflects the complexity and richness of your relationship. Whether it's blending modern and vintage elements or combining cultural influences, let your creativity flow.

Engage in open and collaborative discussions with your partner about your respective visions for the wedding style. This process of mutual exploration and compromise not only strengthens your communication but also ensures that both of you feel a sense of ownership and connection to the chosen style and theme.

Finally, allow flexibility in your vision as it evolves throughout the planning process. Your initial ideas may evolve as you make practical decisions and encounter new inspirations. Embrace the journey of discovery, staying true to the essence of your wedding style while remaining open to the delightful surprises that unfold along the way.

In conclusion, defining your unique wedding style and theme is an invigorating and creative process. It's an opportunity to infuse your celebration with elements that resonate with your personalities and create a visual narrative of your love story. By delving into your personal tastes, incorporating meaningful touches, and staying open to creative possibilities, you're laying the foundation for a wedding style that is authentically and beautifully yours.

Setting Boundaries: Balancing Tradition and Personal Preferences

Setting boundaries when it comes to balancing tradition and personal preferences is a delicate yet empowering aspect of crafting a mindful wedding vision. Wedding planning often involves navigating a myriad of expectations, both internal and external, and finding the balance between honoring traditions and staying true to your unique vision can be a nuanced journey.

Begin by reflecting on the traditions that hold personal significance for you and your partner. Whether it's cultural customs, religious rituals, or family practices, identify the elements that resonate with your values and bring meaning to your celebration. These traditions can serve as the foundation for a wedding that feels deeply rooted in your shared history and identity.

At the same time, acknowledge that not all traditions may align with your personal preferences or the vision you have for your wedding. It's essential to differentiate between traditions that hold genuine meaning for you and those that may be rooted in external expectations. This clarity allows you to set intentional boundaries and make decisions that align with your authentic desires.

Engage in open and honest conversations with key stakeholders, including family members and close friends, about your vision for the wedding. Clearly communicate the aspects of tradition that you wish to prioritize and those where you may choose to deviate.

This open communication fosters understanding and allows others to appreciate the thoughtfulness behind your choices.

Consider incorporating modern interpretations or personal twists into traditional elements. This creative approach allows you to honor traditions while infusing them with a unique and contemporary flair. Whether it's updating the ceremony script, reimagining the dress code, or incorporating personalized vows, these adaptations add a layer of authenticity to your celebration.

Be mindful of cultural or familial expectations, and approach potential deviations from tradition with sensitivity. In some cases, it may be possible to find a middle ground that respects both tradition and personal preferences. Seek compromises that honor the essence of the tradition while aligning with your vision for the celebration.

When faced with conflicting expectations, prioritize what truly resonates with you and your partner. Remember that your wedding is a reflection of your love story, and the decisions you make should feel authentic to both of you. Setting boundaries involves being intentional about the elements that hold significance and politely declining those that may not align with your vision.

Create a list of non-negotiables—elements that are crucial to your vision and should not be compromised. This could include specific aspects of the ceremony, the overall atmosphere, or elements of personal symbolism. Having a clear understanding of your non-negotiables helps you communicate your priorities and make decisions that align with your mindful wedding vision.

Lastly, embrace the concept of blending tradition with personalization. Your wedding is an opportunity to create a celebration that uniquely reflects your partnership. Consider weaving personal touches into traditional elements, such as incorporating family heirlooms, sharing stories during the ceremony, or designing a ceremony space that feels authentically you.

In conclusion, setting boundaries when balancing tradition and personal preferences is about creating a wedding celebration that is a genuine reflection of you and your partner. It's a journey of self-discovery, communication, and creative adaptation. By navigating the delicate dance between tradition and personalization with intention and authenticity, you're crafting a wedding vision that beautifully encapsulates the richness of your love story.

Expressing Individuality in Wedding Choices

Expressing individuality in wedding choices is a delightful and empowering aspect of crafting a mindful wedding vision. Your wedding is a celebration of the unique partnership between you and your significant other, and infusing individuality into every choice ensures that the celebration is a true reflection of your personalities, preferences, and shared journey.

Start by reflecting on your individual and shared interests, passions, and values. Consider what makes your relationship distinctive and what elements hold personal significance for each of you. These insights serve as a foundation for making choices that resonate with your identities and create a celebration that feels authentically yours.

Personalize the ceremony script to reflect your unique love story. Share anecdotes, milestones, and moments that define your journey as a couple. Whether it's the story of how you met, a shared adventure, or the significance of the engagement, weaving personal narratives into the ceremony creates a deeply meaningful and memorable experience for both you and your guests.

Explore alternative options for traditional wedding elements to add a touch of individuality. For instance, instead of a traditional guestbook, consider a creative alternative that aligns with your interests, such as a photo booth guestbook, where guests can leave pictures and notes. Infusing creativity into these details allows you to express your individuality in unexpected and delightful ways.

Consider incorporating elements from your cultural backgrounds, hobbies, or shared experiences into the wedding decor. Whether it's subtle nods in the color scheme, thematic decor that reflects your interests, or specific cultural symbols, these choices not only personalize the celebration but also create a visually rich and meaningful atmosphere.

Personalize your vows to express the unique promises and commitments you're making to each other. Share specific qualities you love about your partner, recall cherished memories, and express your vision for the future together. Writing and exchanging personalized vows is a powerful way to infuse the ceremony with heartfelt sentiments that reflect your individual voices.

Think outside the box when it comes to attire choices. While traditional white dresses and classic suits are timeless, consider adding individual touches that resonate with your personal style. Whether it's incorporating non-traditional colors, unique accessories, or attire that reflects your cultural background, your wedding attire can be a canvas for expressing individuality.

Select a playlist that includes songs that hold personal meaning for both of you. From the song that played during your first dance to tracks that evoke shared memories, curate a musical experience that reflects your musical tastes and the soundtrack of your relationship. Your chosen playlist becomes a personal and emotive element of the celebration.

Consider involving family and friends in the celebration in roles that highlight their unique talents or contributions. Whether it's having a friend perform a musical piece, a family member officiate the ceremony, or loved ones share readings during the service, incorporating these personal touches creates a sense of community and shared joy.

Remember that expressing individuality doesn't necessarily mean deviating from tradition entirely. It's about finding creative ways to infuse elements of your unique personalities into the fabric of the celebration. By embracing the freedom to make choices that authentically represent you and your partner, you're creating a wedding that is not only visually stunning but also deeply meaningful and true to the essence of your love story.

In conclusion, expressing individuality in wedding choices is a celebration of what makes your partnership distinct and special. It's an opportunity to showcase your personalities, values, and shared journey in a way that resonates with both of you. As you make choices that reflect your unique identities, you're not just planning a wedding; you're crafting an experience that beautifully encapsulates the essence of your love story.

Chapter 6: Financial Wellness and Budgeting

Welcome to Chapter 6, where we embark on a practical and essential aspect of wedding planning— Financial Wellness and Budgeting. Planning a wedding involves not just the creativity of crafting a beautiful celebration but also the practicality of managing your finances wisely. In this chapter, we'll explore the art of balancing your wedding dreams with financial realities, ensuring that your journey to the altar is not just joyous but also financially sound.

Financial wellness is a crucial component of your overall well-being, and your wedding is an opportunity to approach financial planning as a couple in a thoughtful and collaborative manner. As you envision the celebration of your love, it's essential to create a realistic budget that aligns with your financial goals and priorities.

We'll delve into the practical aspects of budgeting, breaking down the various components of wedding expenses and providing insights on making informed financial decisions. From venue costs to attire, catering to decorations, this chapter serves as your guide to navigating the financial landscape of wedding planning.

Financial wellness is not just about restriction; it's about mindful decision-making that allows you to allocate resources to the elements that matter most to you. We'll explore strategies for setting priorities within your budget, making trade-offs that align with your values, and finding creative solutions to achieve your vision without compromising financial stability.

This chapter is not just a guide to creating a budget; it's an invitation to cultivate financial communication and teamwork with your partner. Understanding each other's financial goals, discussing spending habits, and working together to make informed decisions are integral aspects of creating a solid financial foundation for your marriage.

Whether you're navigating wedding expenses on a tight budget or have more flexibility, this chapter provides practical tips and insights to help you make the most of your financial resources. We'll explore ways to maximize value, identify potential savings, and approach negotiations with vendors in a way that aligns with your budgetary constraints.

Financial wellness is a journey, and your wedding is just one milestone on this path. By approaching budgeting with intention, mindfulness, and open communication, you're not only creating a beautiful celebration but also laying the groundwork for a financially healthy and harmonious partnership. So, let's embark on this chapter together, weaving the threads of financial wellness into the tapestry of your wedding journey. The road to "I do" is not just about the destination; it's about the steps you take along the way, hand in hand, toward a future of shared prosperity and joy.

Creating a Realistic Wedding Budget

Creating a realistic wedding budget is the cornerstone of financial wellness in your wedding planning journey. While the allure of a dreamy celebration is undeniable, understanding and setting financial boundaries is key to ensuring that your wedding is not just memorable but also financially responsible.

Start by having an open and honest conversation with your partner about your financial goals and priorities. Discuss your individual and shared visions for the wedding, as well as any non-negotiables that may influence the budget. This collaborative approach sets the foundation for a budget that aligns with both your dreams and financial reality.

Identify your funding sources. Determine how much you and your partner can contribute from your savings, and discuss whether family members will be contributing to the wedding budget. Clarifying these funding sources early on allows you to establish a clear financial picture and make informed decisions about your budget.

Consider your overall financial situation, including any existing debts, savings goals, and other financial commitments. Understanding your financial landscape helps you set realistic expectations for your wedding budget and ensures that you're making choices that align with your broader financial well-being.

Research average costs in your location and for your desired level of celebration. While every wedding is unique, having a general understanding of the costs associated with venues, catering, attire, and other elements helps you set realistic expectations and allocate your budget effectively.

Create a detailed budget spreadsheet that outlines all potential expenses. Break down your budget into categories such as venue, catering, attire, decorations, photography, and miscellaneous expenses. Allocate a realistic amount to each category based on your research and priorities.

Be mindful of hidden costs that may arise during the planning process. These can include taxes, service charges, gratuities, and other miscellaneous expenses that may not be immediately apparent. Building a buffer into your budget to account for these unforeseen costs helps you avoid financial stress later in the planning process.

Prioritize your budget based on what matters most to you and your partner. Identify the elements of the wedding that are non-negotiable and allocate a larger portion of your budget to those areas. This ensures that you're directing your resources toward the aspects of the celebration that hold the most significance for you.

Regularly revisit and adjust your budget as needed throughout the planning process. As you make decisions and receive vendor quotes, update your budget spreadsheet to reflect the actual costs incurred. This dynamic approach allows you to stay on top of your financial commitments and make informed adjustments as needed.

Consider enlisting the help of a professional wedding planner who can provide guidance on budgeting and negotiate with vendors on your behalf. While hiring a wedding planner involves an additional expense, their expertise can often result in cost savings, and their knowledge of the industry can help you make informed decisions.

Communicate openly with vendors about your budget constraints. Many vendors are willing to work within your budget and may offer creative solutions to help you achieve your vision without overspending. Clear communication about your financial limits ensures that you're on the same page from the outset.

In conclusion, creating a realistic wedding budget is not just about crunching numbers; it's about aligning your financial goals with your wedding dreams. By approaching budgeting with transparency, collaboration, and a realistic understanding of your financial landscape, you're not just planning a celebration—you're building a foundation for financial wellness in your marriage. As you navigate the budgeting process together, remember that the true value of your wedding lies not in the price tag but in the love, commitment, and joy that you and your partner bring to the celebration.

Smart Spending: Prioritizing and Cutting Costs

Smart spending is a skill that can transform your wedding planning experience, allowing you to prioritize what matters most to you while making informed decisions to stay within your budget. As you navigate the sea of choices and options, consider these strategies for smart spending to ensure that your wedding is both memorable and financially responsible.

Start by identifying your priorities. What aspects of the wedding are most meaningful to you and your partner? Whether it's the venue, photography, attire, or a particular element of the celebration, knowing your priorities allows you to allocate a larger portion of your budget to these key areas. By focusing on what matters most, you create a wedding that is both meaningful and cost-effective.

Consider alternatives and creative solutions for high-cost items. For example, instead of a traditional sit-down dinner, you might opt for a buffet or food stations, which can be more budget-friendly. Similarly, explore alternative venues, such as parks or community spaces, which may offer a charming and cost-effective backdrop for your celebration.

Prioritize spending on elements that have a lasting impact. While flowers and decorations are beautiful, they are temporary. Consider allocating a larger portion of your budget to elements like photography or a live band, which create lasting memories and contribute to the overall atmosphere of your wedding.

Take advantage of off-peak and weekday options. Many vendors offer lower rates for weddings held on weekdays or during off-peak seasons. Choosing a less popular date or time can result in significant cost savings while still allowing you to create a memorable and enjoyable celebration.

Be strategic about timing when booking vendors. Some vendors may offer discounts or special packages for early bookings, especially if you secure their services during the off-peak season. Planning ahead and securing key vendors promptly can contribute to cost savings in the long run.

Explore the world of DIY for certain elements of your wedding. From handmade decorations to DIY invitations, there are numerous opportunities to infuse personal touches into your celebration while also saving on costs. Just be mindful of your time and skill level to ensure that DIY projects enhance rather than add stress to your wedding planning experience.

Negotiate with vendors and explore package deals. Don't be afraid to discuss your budget with vendors and inquire about flexible packages or potential discounts. Many vendors are open to negotiation, especially if it means securing your business. Exploring package deals that include multiple services can also result in cost savings.

Consider renting instead of buying for items like decor, linens, and even attire. Renting can be a cost-effective alternative, especially for items that you may not have a use for after the wedding. This approach allows you to achieve the desired aesthetic without the long-term commitment of ownership.

Explore online resources for budget-friendly options. From pre-loved wedding dresses to affordable decor options, the internet is a treasure trove of budget-friendly resources. Online marketplaces and forums can connect you with sellers offering gently used wedding items, helping you find quality pieces at a fraction of the cost.

Keep in mind that smart spending is not about compromising on the quality or significance of your wedding; it's about making intentional choices that align with your budget and priorities. By thoughtfully navigating the wedding planning process, you can create a celebration that is not only within your financial means but also a true reflection of your love story and values. As you make smart spending decisions, remember that the essence of your wedding lies in the love, joy, and commitment you share with your partner, and these qualities are priceless.

Financial Communication with Your Partner: Building a Strong Foundation

Financial communication is a cornerstone of a strong and harmonious partnership, and your wedding planning journey provides the perfect opportunity to build a solid foundation for this aspect of your relationship. As you navigate the intricacies of budgeting, expenses, and financial decision-making, consider these strategies for fostering open and effective financial communication with your partner.

Start by establishing a safe and judgment-free space for discussing finances. Money can be a sensitive topic, and creating an environment where both you and your partner feel comfortable sharing your thoughts, concerns, and goals is essential. Approach financial discussions with empathy, understanding, and a willingness to listen.

Initiate regular financial check-ins with your partner. Set aside dedicated time to discuss your financial goals, priorities, and any changes in your financial situation. Regular check-ins create an ongoing dialogue about money, preventing surprises and allowing you to make informed decisions together.

Share your individual financial histories, including your attitudes toward money, spending habits, and any financial goals or concerns. Understanding each other's financial perspectives helps build empathy and lays the groundwork for collaborative decision-making. Be open about any debts, savings goals, or financial commitments that may impact your wedding budget and long-term financial plans.

Establish shared financial goals for your wedding and beyond. Discuss your vision for the wedding, financial priorities, and any long-term goals you have as a couple. Whether it's saving for a home, planning for future expenses, or building an emergency fund, aligning your financial goals creates a sense of shared purpose and direction.

Be transparent about your budget and any financial constraints. Discussing the wedding budget openly and honestly allows both partners to have a clear understanding of the financial parameters. This transparency fosters collaboration in making decisions that align with your budgetary constraints while still creating a celebration you both desire.

Assign financial responsibilities based on each other's strengths and preferences. Some individuals may enjoy managing budgets and expenses, while others may find it less enjoyable. Identify tasks that align with each partner's strengths and interests, creating a division of financial responsibilities that feels equitable and manageable.

Discuss financial priorities within the wedding budget. Identify the aspects of the wedding that are most important to each of you. Whether it's the venue, photography, or specific details like personalized decor, understanding each other's priorities allows you to allocate resources in a way that reflects your shared values.

Create a financial plan for after the wedding. Beyond the celebration, discuss your vision for managing finances as a married couple. Consider whether you want to merge accounts, maintain separate accounts, or establish a combination of both. Discuss your approach to saving, investing, and any financial strategies you want to implement for the future.

Be open to compromise and find common ground. Financial discussions may involve differing opinions or priorities, and finding compromises is a key aspect of collaborative decision-making. Approach compromises with a mindset of mutual understanding and a shared commitment to achieving financial goals together.

Consider seeking the guidance of a financial advisor or counselor. Professional support can be beneficial in navigating complex financial decisions. Whether it's creating a comprehensive financial plan, addressing specific concerns, or simply gaining advice on budgeting, a financial professional can provide valuable insights and guidance.

Remember that financial communication is an ongoing process, and the skills you develop during wedding planning will serve you well in your marriage. By fostering open communication, empathy, and a collaborative approach to financial decision-making, you're not just planning a wedding; you're building a foundation for a strong and resilient partnership. As you navigate the complexities of money together, keep in mind that the true wealth of your relationship lies in the love, commitment, and shared dreams you bring to your journey as a couple.

Chapter 7: The Beauty of Self-Care Rituals

Welcome to Chapter 7, where we dive into a topic that is both essential and often overlooked in the whirlwind of wedding planning—The Beauty of Self-Care Rituals. As you embark on the journey to your wedding day, it's easy to get caught up in the excitement and busyness of the process. However, this chapter invites you to pause, take a deep breath, and explore the transformative power of self-care.

In the midst of venue visits, dress fittings, and guest list preparations, it's crucial to prioritize your well-being and embrace self-care as an integral part of the wedding planning experience. Self-care isn't just about pampering; it's a profound act of love and nurturance, allowing you to navigate the planning process with grace, joy, and a sense of inner balance.

Throughout this chapter, we'll unravel the beauty of self-care rituals—simple yet impactful practices that nourish your mind, body, and spirit. From skincare routines to mindfulness exercises, we'll explore a variety of self-care techniques tailored to busy brides-to-be. The goal is not only to enhance your external glow but also to cultivate a radiant and centered inner self as you approach your wedding day.

As you navigate the intricacies of wedding planning, self-care becomes your secret weapon—a source of resilience, clarity, and calm amid the excitement and potential stress. We'll delve into the art of creating personalized self-care rituals that align with your needs and preferences, ensuring that your journey to the altar is not just a checklist of tasks but a transformative and empowering experience.

The Beauty of Self-Care Rituals is an invitation to celebrate and honor yourself throughout the wedding planning process. Whether you're a self-care enthusiast or new to the practice, this chapter provides practical insights, inspiration, and actionable steps to infuse your wedding journey with the beauty of self-care. So, let's embark on this exploration together, embracing the transformative magic that comes from nurturing yourself as you prepare to step into the next beautiful chapter of your life. The journey to self-love, well-being, and a radiant wedding experience begins now.

Skincare and Beauty Prep for the Big Day

As you approach the big day, incorporating a thoughtful skincare and beauty routine into your self-care rituals is a wonderful way to enhance your natural glow and radiate confidence. The months leading up to your wedding provide the perfect opportunity to invest time and care into your skin, ensuring that you look and feel your best on this special occasion.

Start your skincare journey well in advance to allow for a gradual and gentle transformation. Consistency is key, and establishing a routine early on can address specific concerns, such as uneven skin tone, blemishes, or dryness. Consider consulting with a skincare professional to create a customized plan tailored to your skin type and needs.

Hydration is the foundation of healthy and radiant skin. Make it a habit to drink plenty of water throughout the day to keep your skin hydrated from the inside out. Additionally, choose a moisturizer that suits your skin type and use it consistently to maintain suppleness and prevent dryness.

Regular cleansing is essential to remove impurities, makeup, and environmental pollutants that can accumulate on your skin. Find a gentle cleanser that suits your skin type, and cleanse your face morning and night. Incorporating exfoliation into your routine once or twice a week helps to slough off dead skin cells and promote a smoother complexion.

Protecting your skin from the sun is crucial, especially as you prepare for outdoor events and photo sessions. Use a broad-spectrum sunscreen with at least SPF 30 daily, even on cloudy days. This simple step not only prevents sun damage but also contributes to an even skin tone.

Consider scheduling professional skincare treatments in the months leading up to your wedding.

Facials, microdermabrasion, or chemical peels can address specific concerns and give your skin a rejuvenated and refreshed appearance. Discuss your timeline and goals with a skincare professional to create a plan that aligns with your wedding date.

Eye care is often overlooked but can make a significant difference in your overall appearance. Invest in a hydrating and nourishing eye cream to address puffiness, dark circles, and fine lines. Consistent use can brighten and revitalize the delicate skin around your eyes.

Nourish your skin from the inside by incorporating a balanced and nutrient-rich diet. Foods rich in antioxidants, such as fruits, vegetables, and omega-3 fatty acids, contribute to a healthy complexion. Consider consulting with a nutritionist to optimize your diet for glowing skin.

Prioritize stress management as part of your beauty prep. Stress can manifest in various ways, including on your skin. Incorporate relaxation techniques such as meditation, deep breathing, or yoga into your routine to promote overall well-being and a calm, radiant complexion.

In the weeks leading up to your wedding, be mindful of introducing new skincare products. Stick to familiar products that have been tried and tested to avoid potential reactions or sensitivities. If you're considering trying something new, do a patch test well in advance to ensure compatibility with your skin.

Remember that the goal of your skincare and beauty prep is not perfection but a radiant and confident version of yourself. Embrace the unique qualities of your skin and focus on enhancing its natural beauty. Your wedding day is a celebration of love, and your glow comes from the happiness and excitement that radiate from within.

In conclusion, skincare and beauty prep is a delightful and pampering aspect of your wedding self-care rituals. By establishing a consistent routine, addressing specific concerns, and nourishing your skin from the inside out, you're not just preparing for the big day—you're cultivating a lifelong commitment to the health and well-being of your skin. As you embark on this journey, relish in the moments of self-care, and let the beauty of your skin reflect the joy and anticipation of the beautiful celebration ahead.

Hair Care and Styling Tips

Your wedding day is not just an ordinary day—it's a momentous occasion where every detail, including your hair, deserves thoughtful attention. As you prepare to say "I do," incorporating a dedicated hair care and styling routine into your self-care rituals ensures that your tresses are radiant, healthy, and styled to perfection on the big day.

Begin your hair care journey well in advance of your wedding date. Like skincare, consistent care is essential for achieving the desired results. If you have specific hair concerns, whether it's dryness, frizz, or lack of volume, consider consulting with a professional stylist to create a personalized plan tailored to your hair type and goals.

Invest in a quality shampoo and conditioner that suits your hair type and addresses any specific needs. Whether your hair is curly, straight, thin, or thick, choosing products formulated for your unique texture helps maintain its health and vitality. If you plan to change your hair color, start the process gradually to achieve the desired shade without compromising the health of your hair.

Regular trims are the secret to maintaining healthy and vibrant locks. Schedule trims every few months to prevent split ends and promote overall hair health. Trimming also ensures that your hair looks fresh and polished on your wedding day, especially if you're growing it out for a specific style.

Deep conditioning treatments can work wonders for nourishing your hair and addressing specific concerns. Consider incorporating a hydrating mask into your routine once a week to add moisture, improve elasticity, and enhance the overall condition of your hair. This pampering ritual becomes even more crucial as you approach your wedding date.

If you're planning to change your hairstyle for the wedding, schedule a trial with your hairstylist well in advance. This allows you to experiment with different styles, find the one that complements your features and dress, and make any adjustments as needed. The trial also gives you peace of mind, knowing exactly how your hair will look on the big day.

Consider the overall theme and vibe of your wedding when choosing a hairstyle. Whether you envision a romantic updo, loose waves, or a sleek ponytail, your hairstyle should complement the overall aesthetic of your celebration. Share your wedding theme and dress details with your hairstylist to ensure a cohesive and harmonious look.

Hair accessories can add a touch of elegance and personal style to your wedding look. Whether it's a delicate headpiece, a floral crown, or vintage-inspired hairpins, the right accessory can elevate your hairstyle and tie together the overall bridal ensemble. Choose accessories that resonate with your style and the theme of your wedding.

As your wedding day approaches, avoid drastic changes to your hair. Stick to the routine and products that have worked well for you during the planning process to minimize the risk of unexpected results. If you're considering a new color or haircut, do so well in advance to allow time for adjustments.

On the day of your wedding, trust your hairstylist and enjoy the process of being pampered. Provide any hair accessories, veils, or other items you plan to incorporate into your hairstyle, and communicate openly with your stylist about your preferences. This collaboration ensures that your hairstyle aligns seamlessly with your vision for the day.

Remember, your wedding hairstyle is an expression of your personality and style. Whether you choose a classic updo, romantic curls, or a chic bob, the key is to feel comfortable and confident in your choice. Your hair is a beautiful canvas, and with the right care and styling, it becomes a stunning complement to your radiant bridal look. As you embark on your hair care and styling journey, relish in the joy of preparing for the day you'll cherish forever.

Mindful Grooming: Creating a Routine that Boosts Confidence

Grooming isn't just a routine; it's a powerful form of self-care that contributes to your overall well-being and confidence. As you prepare for your wedding day, incorporating mindful grooming practices into your routine is a wonderful way to enhance your natural charm and radiate confidence. This section explores the art of mindful grooming—creating a routine that not only boosts your external appearance but also nurtures your inner sense of well-being.

Begin with the basics—regular skin care. Cleansing your face with a gentle yet effective cleanser removes impurities and sets the foundation for healthy skin. Follow up with a moisturizer suitable for your skin type to keep your skin hydrated and balanced. These simple steps, when done consistently, contribute to a clear and vibrant complexion.

Consider incorporating a shaving routine that suits your skin's needs. Whether you prefer a clean shave or a well-groomed beard, maintaining your facial hair contributes to a polished and put-together appearance. Invest in quality shaving products and take your time to avoid irritation, allowing the grooming process to become a mindful and enjoyable ritual.

Nail care is often overlooked but plays a significant role in your overall grooming. Regularly trimming your nails, cleaning under the nail beds, and using a moisturizing hand cream contribute to a neat and well-maintained appearance. If you're open to it, consider a professional manicure for a polished finish.

Hair grooming goes beyond just the cut; it's about maintaining healthy and well-styled hair. Regular shampooing and conditioning keep your hair looking fresh and vibrant. If you have a specific hairstyle in mind for your wedding, discuss it with your hairstylist and ensure you're on a maintenance schedule that aligns with your desired look.

Mindful grooming extends to your wardrobe choices. Invest time in curating a wardrobe that reflects your style and makes you feel confident. Whether it's a well-tailored suit, stylish accessories, or comfortable yet elegant casual wear, your clothing choices contribute to your overall grooming and presentation.

Consider skincare treatments that target specific concerns. If you have concerns such as acne, uneven skin tone, or signs of aging, consult with a skincare professional to explore treatment options. These treatments can be integrated into your grooming routine in the months leading up to your wedding, contributing to a refined and refreshed appearance.

Maintaining good posture is a subtle yet impactful aspect of grooming. Stand tall with your shoulders back, conveying confidence and self-assurance. Practicing good posture not only enhances your physical presence but also positively influences your mindset.

Mindful grooming involves being present in the moment and savoring the experience. Whether you're applying skincare products, shaving, or selecting your outfit, take the time to enjoy the process. This mindful approach transforms grooming from a mundane task into a self-care ritual that nurtures your body and spirit.

In the days leading up to your wedding, schedule a grooming session to ensure you look and feel your best. Whether it's a haircut, a beard trim, or a relaxing skincare treatment, these final touches contribute to a groomed and confident appearance. Communicate openly with your grooming professionals about your preferences and any specific details related to your wedding look.

Remember that mindful grooming is a journey, not a destination. The goal is not perfection but the authentic expression of your unique style and personality. As you embrace mindful grooming practices, you're not just preparing for a day; you're cultivating a mindset of self-care that will serve you well beyond the wedding. Your confident and well-groomed self is a reflection of the joy and anticipation you bring to the celebration, and that radiance is truly timeless.

Chapter 8: Healthy Eating Habits

Welcome to Chapter 8, where we explore the delightful world of Healthy Eating Habits—a cornerstone of self-care that extends far beyond the wedding day. As you navigate the excitement of planning your celebration, nourishing your body with wholesome and balanced meals becomes a key component of your overall well-being. This chapter is not about strict diets or restrictions; it's a celebration of delicious, nourishing food that supports your health and vitality.

In the midst of tastings, menu planning, and perhaps a few indulgences, maintaining a focus on healthy eating is an empowering choice that contributes to your energy, mood, and overall sense of well-being. Healthy eating isn't just about the physical aspects of wellness; it's about savoring the joy of good food and creating sustainable habits that extend into your married life.

Throughout this chapter, we'll embark on a journey to discover practical tips, flavorful recipes, and mindful approaches to healthy eating. From understanding the nutritional needs of your body to navigating the nuances of wedding-related events, we'll explore how to strike a balance between savoring the culinary delights of your wedding journey and nourishing your body with intention.

Healthy Eating Habits is an invitation to embrace a positive and balanced relationship with food as you prepare for your wedding. We'll debunk common myths, share practical strategies for incorporating nutrient-rich foods into your diet, and celebrate the pleasure of enjoying meals that both delight your taste buds and support your well-being.

Whether you're a seasoned health enthusiast or just beginning to explore the world of nutrition, this chapter offers a friendly and inclusive guide to making food choices that align with your goals and values. So, let's dive into the delicious realm of Healthy Eating Habits, where nourishment and joy go hand in hand. As you embark on this culinary adventure, may your plates be filled with goodness, your taste buds dance with delight, and your journey to the altar be fueled by the energy of wholesome and delicious choices.

Nourishing Your Body for Increased Energy

Fueling your body with the right nutrients is a transformative act of self-care, especially during the exhilarating yet demanding process of wedding planning. In this section, we'll explore the concept of nourishing your body for increased energy—a key ingredient for navigating the to-do lists, meetings, and celebrations with vitality and joy.

Start by embracing a balanced and varied diet that includes a rainbow of fruits, vegetables, whole grains, lean proteins, and healthy fats. Each of these food groups brings unique nutritional benefits, providing your body with a spectrum of vitamins, minerals, and energy sources. Aim for a well-rounded plate that reflects the diversity of nutrient-rich foods available to you.

Breakfast, often hailed as the most important meal of the day, sets the tone for your energy levels. Choose a breakfast that combines complex carbohydrates, protein, and healthy fats to provide sustained energy. Options like whole-grain toast with avocado and eggs, or a smoothie with fruits, greens, and a source of protein, are excellent choices.

Snacking can be a strategic tool for maintaining energy levels throughout the day. Opt for snacks that combine carbohydrates and protein, such as a handful of nuts with fruit or yogurt with granola. These combinations help stabilize blood sugar levels and provide a sustained release of energy.

Stay hydrated by drinking plenty of water throughout the day. Dehydration can lead to fatigue and decreased alertness, so make it a habit to carry a water bottle and sip regularly. If you find plain water unappealing, infuse it with slices of citrus, cucumber, or herbs for a refreshing twist.

Consider the timing of your meals to maintain a steady flow of energy. Instead of relying on large, infrequent meals, aim for smaller, more frequent meals and snacks. This approach helps prevent energy crashes and provides a continuous source of fuel for your body.

Incorporate energy-boosting foods into your diet, such as those rich in iron, magnesium, and B-vitamins. Iron-rich foods like lean meats, beans, and leafy greens support oxygen transport in the body, while magnesium-rich foods like nuts, seeds, and whole grains contribute to energy metabolism. B-vitamins, found in foods like eggs, dairy, and leafy greens, play a role in converting food into energy.

Consider the impact of caffeine on your energy levels. While moderate caffeine intake can provide a temporary energy boost, excessive consumption may lead to energy crashes and disrupt sleep. Be mindful of your sensitivity to caffeine and choose beverages like green tea for a gentler, sustained lift.

Prioritize adequate sleep as a fundamental pillar of sustained energy. Quality sleep allows your body to recharge, repair, and prepare for the demands of the day. Aim for seven to nine hours of sleep each night, and establish a consistent sleep routine to support overall well-being.

Regular physical activity is a powerful ally in boosting energy levels. Engage in activities you enjoy, whether it's a brisk walk, a dance class, or yoga. Physical activity not only enhances energy but also contributes to overall mood and well-being.

Mindful eating is an integral part of nourishing your body for increased energy. Pay attention to your body's hunger and fullness cues, savor the flavors of your meals, and eat without distractions. This mindful approach allows you to enjoy your food fully and enhances the satisfaction derived from your meals.

In conclusion, nourishing your body for increased energy is a holistic and joyous endeavor. As you embark on this culinary journey, remember that the goal is not perfection but a sustainable and enjoyable approach to fueling your body. By incorporating nutrient-rich foods, staying hydrated, and prioritizing rest and physical activity, you're not just preparing for your wedding—you're cultivating habits that contribute to a vibrant and energized life. So, let the journey to increased energy be as delightful as the dishes you savor, and may each bite bring you closer to the radiant vitality you deserve.

The Role of Hydration in Overall Well-Being

Hydration is not just a simple act of drinking water; it's a cornerstone of overall well-being that profoundly impacts your physical and mental vitality. In this section, we'll delve into the essential role of hydration—why it matters, how it supports your body, and practical tips for maintaining optimal hydration, especially during the dynamic and often hectic period of wedding planning.

Water is the unsung hero of your body's functions, playing a vital role in nearly every physiological process. From regulating body temperature to aiding digestion and supporting nutrient transport, adequate hydration is the key to ensuring your body operates at its best.

During the whirlwind of wedding planning, it's easy to overlook the importance of staying hydrated. Yet, dehydration can manifest in subtle ways, impacting your energy levels, cognitive function, and overall sense of well-being. To stay ahead of the game, make a conscious effort to prioritize hydration throughout the day.

Start your morning with a refreshing glass of water. After a night of sleep, your body is naturally in a mildly dehydrated state. Rehydrate by drinking a glass of water upon waking to kickstart your metabolism and replenish fluid levels.

Carry a reusable water bottle with you throughout the day. Having water readily available makes it more likely that you'll sip consistently. Whether you're at work, running errands, or attending wedding-related appointments, having a water bottle by your side serves as a visual reminder to stay hydrated.

Listen to your body's thirst signals. Thirst is a natural indicator that your body needs water. Rather than waiting until you feel parched, sip water regularly to maintain a steady level of hydration. If you find it challenging to remember, set reminders on your phone or incorporate water breaks into your routine.

Incorporate hydrating foods into your diet. Fruits and vegetables, such as watermelon, cucumber, and oranges, have high water content and contribute to your overall fluid intake. Including these hydrating foods in your meals and snacks enhances your hydration efforts.

Consider the impact of caffeinated and alcoholic beverages on hydration. While moderate consumption of coffee, tea, and alcohol is generally acceptable, excessive intake can contribute to dehydration. Balance these beverages with water and be mindful of their effects on your overall fluid balance.

Infuse your water with flavor. If plain water feels uninspiring, add a splash of natural flavor with slices of citrus, berries, or herbs like mint. Experiment with different combinations to create refreshing and enjoyable infused water options.

Pay attention to the color of your urine. A pale yellow color indicates proper hydration, while dark yellow or amber may signal dehydration. Monitoring the color of your urine provides a simple and practical gauge of your hydration status.

Recognize the signs of dehydration, which can include fatigue, dizziness, headache, and dry skin. If you experience these symptoms, prioritize rehydration by sipping water consistently and, if needed, incorporating hydrating snacks into your routine.

In the weeks leading up to your wedding, make hydration a non-negotiable part of your self-care routine. Proper hydration contributes to clear skin, increased energy, and a heightened sense of well-being—qualities you'll undoubtedly want to radiate on your special day.

As you navigate the myriad details of wedding planning, let hydration be your steadfast companion. The simple act of drinking water is a powerful form of self-care that nourishes your body, supports your well-being, and ensures you approach your wedding day with a radiant and hydrated glow. So, raise your water bottle as a toast to the beauty of staying hydrated, and may each sip be a refreshing reminder of the vibrant health and joy you bring to every moment of this extraordinary journey.

Mindful Eating: Balancing Indulgence and Nutrition

Mindful eating is a practice that transcends the act of consuming food; it's a way of cultivating a deeper connection with what you eat, savoring the flavors, and appreciating the nourishment it provides to your body. As you navigate the culinary landscape of wedding planning, mindful eating becomes a valuable tool for balancing indulgence and nutrition.

At its core, mindful eating is about being present and fully engaged with your meals. It involves paying attention to the sensory experience of eating—savoring the tastes, appreciating the textures, and acknowledging the nourishment each bite offers. This practice encourages a more intentional and conscious relationship with food, fostering a greater understanding of your body's hunger and fullness cues.

During the excitement of wedding planning, it's common to encounter a variety of food-related events, from tastings and celebrations to the occasional indulgence. Mindful eating allows you to approach these moments with a sense of balance and awareness, preventing mindless overeating while still savoring the joy of delicious meals.

Start by tuning into your body's hunger signals. Before reaching for a snack or meal, take a moment to assess whether you're truly hungry or simply responding to external cues. Mindful eating encourages eating when your body signals hunger, fostering a more intuitive and responsive approach to nourishment.

Create a mindful eating environment by minimizing distractions. Turn off the TV, put away electronic devices, and focus on the act of eating. This intentional setting allows you to fully appreciate the sensory experience of your meals, promoting a more satisfying and enjoyable eating experience.

Savor each bite by chewing slowly and deliberately. Mindful eating is not a race; it's an opportunity to engage with your food fully. Chewing slowly not only enhances the enjoyment of your meals but also allows your body to recognize feelings of fullness more effectively.

Recognize the difference between physical hunger and emotional cravings. Mindful eating encourages you to explore the underlying reasons for eating, whether it's true hunger, boredom, stress, or other emotional triggers. By acknowledging these cues, you can make choices that align with your true needs.

Practice portion control by serving reasonable portions and being mindful of seconds. Mindful eating is not about restriction but about listening to your body's signals. When you're attuned to your hunger and fullness cues, you naturally find a balance that suits your individual needs.

Embrace the concept of "gentle nutrition." Rather than fixating on rigid dietary rules, focus on making choices that nourish your body and align with your overall well-being. This approach allows for flexibility and enjoyment in your food choices while prioritizing nutrient-dense options.

Navigate indulgent moments with a sense of mindfulness. Whether it's a wedding cake tasting or a celebratory meal, approach these occasions with a balance of enjoyment and awareness. Allow yourself to savor the flavors without guilt, and be mindful of your body's signals throughout the experience.

Reflect on your eating habits without judgment. Mindful eating encourages self-compassion and curiosity rather than criticism. If you find yourself making less-than-ideal choices, approach it as an opportunity to learn and adjust rather than a reason for guilt or shame.

As you integrate mindful eating into your wedding journey, consider it a lifelong practice that extends beyond the celebrations. Cultivating a mindful approach to eating enhances your overall relationship with food, promotes a positive body image, and contributes to a sense of balance and well-being. So, let each bite be a celebration of nourishment and joy, and may the practice of mindful eating enrich your wedding experience with a delightful and harmonious connection to the food you love.

Chapter 9: Self-Care Spa Days and Retreats

Welcome to Chapter 9, a delightful exploration into the world of Self-Care Spa Days and Retreats—an oasis of relaxation and rejuvenation amidst the whirlwind of wedding planning. As you navigate the myriad details of creating your dream celebration, this chapter invites you to take a pause, indulge in moments of self-care, and embrace the therapeutic bliss of spa-inspired rituals.

Wedding planning, with its joyous moments and occasional stresses, can be a transformative journey. Amidst the excitement of selecting venues, curating guest lists, and envisioning your perfect day, it's easy to lose sight of the importance of caring for yourself. That's where Self-Care Spa Days and Retreats come in—a sanctuary for replenishing your mind, body, and spirit.

In this chapter, we'll embark on a guided exploration of spa-inspired self-care, from creating your own at-home spa experiences to considering the allure of wellness retreats. Imagine a world where tranquility reigns, and each moment is an invitation to unwind and revitalize. Whether you're seeking a quiet escape within the comfort of your home or contemplating a rejuvenating getaway, Self-Care Spa Days and Retreats are crafted to cater to your well-being.

We'll delve into the art of pampering, from DIY face masks to the therapeutic benefits of massages and holistic treatments. Discover how to curate spa days that align with your preferences and bring a sense of calm to your wedding journey. Additionally, we'll explore the enchanting realm of wellness retreats—a chance to immerse yourself in serene environments, surrounded by nature and dedicated to self-discovery.

Amid the hustle and bustle of planning a wedding, this chapter serves as a gentle reminder that your well-being deserves a place in the spotlight. Whether you're drawn to the tranquility of a candlelit bath, the soothing touch of a skilled masseuse, or the serenity of a retreat nestled in nature, Self-Care Spa Days and Retreats offer a holistic approach to rejuvenation.

So, let the pages of this chapter be a guide to creating moments of serenity and self-indulgence. As you delve into the world of spa-inspired self-care, may you find joy in the simplicity of a pampering routine and the profound benefits of prioritizing your well-being. Your journey to the altar is not just about the destination; it's a celebration of the radiant, well-nurtured bride-to-be you are. So, slip into your metaphorical robe of relaxation, and let the spa-inspired self-care journey begin.

Planning Relaxing Pre-Wedding Spa Days

In the midst of wedding planning, taking a pause to indulge in a pre-wedding spa day can be a luxurious and rejuvenating experience. These intentional moments of self-care not only offer physical relaxation but also contribute to mental clarity and a sense of overall well-being. As you embark on planning your own pre-wedding spa day, consider it an opportunity to unwind, recharge, and bask in the anticipation of your special day.

Start by setting the scene. Whether you're creating a spa day at home or booking a day at a professional spa, ambiance plays a crucial role. Select soothing music, light candles, and create an environment that evokes tranquility. This simple yet effective step sets the stage for a spa experience that transports you away from the hustle and bustle of wedding preparations.

Consider inviting close friends or family to join you. A pre-wedding spa day becomes even more special when shared with loved ones. Whether it's your bridesmaids, family members, or even your partner, the shared experience adds an element of connection and joy to the day. If you prefer solitude, embrace the opportunity for some quiet, introspective moments.

Craft a personalized spa menu tailored to your preferences. If you're at home, this could include DIY face masks, scrubs, and hair treatments using natural ingredients. If you're at a spa, explore the menu of services and choose those that align with your relaxation goals. Massages, facials, and body treatments are popular choices that provide both physical and mental rejuvenation.

Indulge in a warm bath infused with calming ingredients. Whether you're in your own tub or at a spa, a bath is a timeless ritual that promotes relaxation. Consider adding Epsom salts, essential oils, or bath bombs to enhance the soothing experience. Allow yourself to unwind and let the warm water melt away any tension.

Prioritize skincare with a tailored facial routine. If you're at home, explore skincare products that suit your skin type and address any specific concerns. If you're at a spa, indulge in a professional facial that nourishes and revitalizes your skin. The glow from a well-crafted skincare routine is a beautiful addition to your wedding radiance.

Incorporate mindfulness and relaxation techniques. Whether it's guided meditation, deep breathing exercises, or gentle yoga, integrating mindfulness into your spa day enhances the overall experience. Take moments to be present, letting go of wedding-related thoughts and embracing the tranquility of the spa environment.

Stay hydrated throughout the day. Hydration is a key component of any spa experience. Sip on water, herbal teas, or infused waters to nourish your body from the inside out. Proper hydration complements the benefits of spa treatments and contributes to a radiant, healthy glow.

Choose comfortable attire that allows you to fully relax. Whether you're in a plush robe at a spa or your favorite cozy loungewear at home, the right attire enhances the comfort of your spa day. Embrace loose, breathable fabrics that allow you to move freely and fully enjoy the experience.

Take time for reflection and gratitude. As your pre-wedding spa day unfolds, pause to reflect on the journey that has led you to this moment. Express gratitude for the love and support surrounding you. These moments of reflection add a meaningful dimension to your spa day, infusing it with a sense of joy and appreciation.

In conclusion, planning a pre-wedding spa day is a gift to yourself—an intentional break from the hustle of wedding preparations to focus on your well-being. Whether you're creating a spa oasis at home or indulging in professional treatments, these moments of self-care contribute to a sense of calm and radiance. So, as you plan your pre-wedding spa day, may it be a celebration of the beautiful journey you're on, and may the relaxation and joy you experience become cherished memories as you approach your special day.

The Benefits of a Wellness Retreat: A Break from Wedding Stress

Amid the flurry of wedding preparations, the idea of a wellness retreat may feel like a luxurious escape. However, beyond the allure of a vacation, wellness retreats offer a myriad of benefits that extend far beyond relaxation. Let's delve into why a wellness retreat can be a transformative break from wedding stress, providing not only physical rejuvenation but also mental and emotional well-being.

First and foremost, a wellness retreat provides a change of scenery. Stepping away from the familiar surroundings of wedding planning allows you to detach from the to-do lists, decisions, and potential stressors. Whether you choose a tranquil nature retreat, a beachfront escape, or a holistic wellness center, the new environment sets the stage for a mental reset.

One of the key benefits of a wellness retreat is the opportunity to unplug. In the digital age, constant connectivity can contribute to wedding-related stress. A retreat offers a chance to disconnect from emails, notifications, and the demands of technology. Embracing a digital detox allows you to fully immerse yourself in the present moment, fostering a sense of mindfulness and tranquility.

Wellness retreats often emphasize holistic well-being, addressing not only physical health but also mental and emotional balance. Through a variety of activities such as yoga, meditation, and mindfulness practices, you gain tools to manage stress, cultivate inner peace, and approach challenges with a centered mindset. These practices become invaluable resources as you navigate the highs and lows of wedding planning.

Engaging in physical activities during a wellness retreat contributes to both physical fitness and stress relief. Whether it's hiking, yoga classes, or rejuvenating spa treatments, these activities promote relaxation, improve mood, and release tension stored in the body. The blend of movement and relaxation creates a holistic approach to well-being that complements the demands of wedding preparations.

Wellness retreats often prioritize healthy eating, providing nourishing meals that support energy levels and overall vitality. A break from wedding-related indulgences allows you to focus on nutritious, delicious food that not only fuels your body but also contributes to a sense of well-being. This mindful approach to eating becomes a refreshing contrast to the occasional indulgences of wedding planning.

Connecting with like-minded individuals at a wellness retreat can be a profound aspect of the experience. Sharing stories, challenges, and laughter with others who may be on similar journeys fosters a sense of community and support. These connections become a source of inspiration and encouragement, offering perspectives that extend beyond the world of wedding preparations.

A wellness retreat offers the luxury of time—time for self-reflection, self-care, and intentional relaxation. Whether you're engaging in a silent meditation walk, journaling by a quiet stream, or simply lounging by a pool, the unstructured time allows you to tune into your own needs and desires. This intentional focus on self-care becomes a valuable asset as you return to the wedding planning process with renewed energy and clarity.

The benefits of a wellness retreat extend beyond the retreat itself, influencing how you approach wedding planning and daily life. The practices and insights gained during the retreat become tools for self-care, stress management, and maintaining a sense of balance. As you weave these practices into your routine, you carry the benefits of the retreat into your wedding journey and beyond.

In conclusion, a wellness retreat is not just a vacation; it's a strategic investment in your well-being. As you temporarily step away from wedding stress, you gift yourself the opportunity to recharge physically, mentally, and emotionally. The retreat becomes a sanctuary for self-discovery, relaxation, and the cultivation of habits that contribute to a balanced and joyful approach to wedding planning and life. So, whether you're drawn to the mountains, the sea, or a tranquil wellness center, may your wellness retreat be a transformative pause on your journey to the altar, and may the benefits resonate long after the retreat concludes.

DIY Self-Care Rituals for Home

Creating your own DIY self-care rituals at home is a delightful and accessible way to infuse your wedding planning journey with moments of tranquility and pampering. These rituals, designed to cater to your unique preferences and needs, offer a sense of solace and rejuvenation within the comfort of your own space. Let's explore the art of crafting personalized self-care rituals that become cherished moments in your pre-wedding routine.

Begin by establishing a dedicated self-care space. Whether it's a cozy corner of your bedroom, a serene bathroom retreat, or even a designated spot in your living room, having a space devoted to self-care creates a tangible invitation to unwind. Arrange soft blankets, cushions, or candles to evoke a sense of comfort and serenity.

Consider incorporating aromatherapy into your self-care rituals. Essential oils like lavender, chamomile, and eucalyptus can be transformative in creating a soothing atmosphere. Whether through diffusers, candles, or sachets, the gentle scents contribute to relaxation and serve as a cue to shift into a more mindful state.

Indulge in a DIY spa day with homemade face masks, scrubs, and hair treatments. Crafting these concoctions from natural ingredients allows you to tailor them to your skin and hair needs. Ingredients like honey, yogurt, avocado, and oats can be combined to create nourishing masks that leave your skin glowing and your hair luxuriously soft.

Integrate mindfulness practices into your self-care routine. This could include guided meditation, deep breathing exercises, or gentle stretching. Mindfulness helps anchor you in the present moment, allowing you to let go of wedding-related thoughts and embrace the tranquility of your self-care ritual.

Embrace the therapeutic benefits of a warm bath. Adding Epsom salts, bath bombs, or a few drops of your favorite essential oil can elevate the experience. Let the warm water soothe your muscles, calm your mind, and create a sense of luxurious relaxation. Consider playing soft music or enjoying a podcast for an added layer of serenity.

Invest in high-quality skincare products that align with your skin's needs. A thoughtful skincare routine becomes a form of self-care, allowing you to nurture your skin and indulge in moments of self-love. Cleansing, toning, moisturizing, and incorporating serums can be both beneficial for your skin and a calming ritual.

Explore the world of relaxation through tea. Brewing a cup of your favorite herbal tea becomes a ritual in itself. The act of slowly sipping a warm beverage can be a meditative practice, allowing you to savor the flavors and create a moment of quiet reflection.

Engage your senses through music or soundscape selections. Create playlists that evoke the atmosphere you desire, whether it's calming instrumental melodies, nature sounds, or your favorite tunes. The auditory backdrop enhances the overall ambiance of your self-care ritual.

Unplug from electronic devices during your self-care time. Set boundaries around screen time to fully immerse yourself in the present moment. This intentional break from technology contributes to a sense of mindfulness and allows you to connect more deeply with the soothing elements of your ritual.

Capture the essence of your self-care moments through journaling. Reflect on how these rituals make you feel, jot down any insights, or simply document the aspects of your self-care routine that bring you joy. The act of journaling becomes a form of self-expression and a way to track the evolution of your self-care journey.

In conclusion, DIY self-care rituals at home are a personal and heartfelt way to infuse your wedding planning journey with moments of rejuvenation. As you craft these rituals, remember that they are a celebration of self-love and an acknowledgment of the importance of your well-being on this transformative journey. May your DIY self-care moments be filled with serenity, joy, and the nurturing embrace of rituals designed uniquely for you.

Chapter 10: Balancing Work and Wedding Planning

Chapter 10 welcomes you to the delicate dance of Balancing Work and Wedding Planning—a chapter designed to support you in navigating the intricacies of juggling a busy professional life while orchestrating the wedding of your dreams. As you embark on this dual journey, we'll explore practical strategies, time-management techniques, and self-care practices that harmonize the demands of work and the joys of wedding planning.

The workplace can be a bustling arena of deadlines, meetings, and projects, and the prospect of adding wedding planning to the mix might initially seem daunting. Fear not! This chapter is your guide to maintaining equilibrium, ensuring that both your professional and personal spheres coexist harmoniously.

We'll delve into strategies for effective time management, helping you carve out dedicated moments for wedding-related tasks without compromising your professional commitments. From creating detailed schedules to leveraging productivity tools, you'll discover methods that streamline your workflow and allow you to savor the wedding planning process without feeling overwhelmed.

Balancing work and wedding planning is not only about managing time but also about nurturing your well-being. We'll explore self-care practices tailored to the demands of a busy schedule, ensuring that you navigate both realms with grace and resilience. From mindful breaks to strategies for preventing burnout, this chapter emphasizes the importance of self-care as a foundational element in the art of balance.

Furthermore, we'll address effective communication strategies, both at work and with wedding vendors, ensuring that you maintain transparency and openness in both spheres. From setting realistic expectations with colleagues to fostering clear communication with your wedding team, you'll learn to navigate potential challenges with finesse.

As you embark on the journey of Balancing Work and Wedding Planning, envision it as a dance where each step is purposeful, and the rhythm adapts to the demands of the music. Through practical insights, supportive strategies, and a touch of humor, this chapter is designed to empower you to embrace the dual roles of professional and bride-to-be with confidence, poise, and a healthy dose of self-care. So, let the music play, and let the dance of balancing work and wedding planning begin!

Time Management Strategies for Working Brides

Navigating the dual roles of a working professional and a bride-to-be requires a delicate balance, and effective time management becomes your trusty companion in this intricate dance. As you embark on this journey, consider time not as an elusive resource but as a flexible ally that, with thoughtful planning and a touch of creativity, can be harnessed to serve both your professional and wedding planning needs.

Begin by embracing the power of prioritization. In the world of work and wedding planning, not all tasks are created equal. Assess your to-do list and identify the high-priority items that require immediate attention. By focusing on the most crucial tasks first, you ensure that you make significant progress even on your busiest days.

Leverage the magic of calendars and planners. These tools are your allies in the realm of time management. Invest time in creating a comprehensive calendar that encompasses both work and wedding-related deadlines. Sync your professional and personal calendars to avoid scheduling conflicts and ensure that you allocate time for both aspects of your life.

Consider adopting the "time blocking" technique. This involves dedicating specific blocks of time to different categories of tasks. For instance, designate mornings for work-related responsibilities and afternoons for wedding planning tasks. This intentional division allows you to immerse yourself fully in each role without feeling pulled in multiple directions simultaneously.

Learn to gracefully say "no" when necessary. As a working bride, your plate is undoubtedly full. While the excitement of wedding planning might make you inclined to take on additional responsibilities, it's crucial to recognize your limits. Politely decline tasks or commitments that may stretch you thin and compromise your well-being.

Embrace the power of delegation. In both your professional and wedding planning spheres, identify tasks that can be effectively delegated. Whether it's assigning work responsibilities to team members or enlisting the help of friends and family for wedding tasks, delegation allows you to share the load and maintain your equilibrium.

Implement the two-minute rule. If a task requires less than two minutes to complete, tackle it immediately. This simple yet effective rule prevents small tasks from accumulating and becoming overwhelming. By addressing quick tasks promptly, you maintain a sense of order and prevent them from adding unnecessary stress to your schedule.

Establish designated "wedding-free" zones. While wedding planning is undoubtedly exciting, it's essential to create boundaries to prevent it from infiltrating every aspect of your life. Designate specific times or areas where wedding discussions and tasks are off-limits, allowing you to fully immerse yourself in work or enjoy moments of personal relaxation.

Integrate self-care into your daily routine. Recognize that effective time management extends beyond tasks and deadlines—it also involves nurturing your well-being. Schedule moments of self-care throughout your week, whether it's a brief walk, a mindfulness practice, or simply taking a break to recharge. Prioritizing self-care contributes to sustained energy and resilience.

As you navigate the intricacies of balancing work and wedding planning, remember that time management is not about squeezing more tasks into your day but about optimizing the time you have. By aligning your priorities, utilizing organizational tools, and embracing strategies that promote balance, you empower yourself to gracefully navigate both worlds. Let time management be your supportive companion in this journey, ensuring that you not only meet your professional and wedding planning commitments but also savor each moment of this transformative chapter in your life.

Communicating Boundaries with Employers and Colleagues

Navigating the delicate balance between work and wedding planning involves not only managing your time effectively but also establishing clear and respectful communication with your employers and colleagues. Articulating your boundaries is a key component of maintaining equilibrium, ensuring that both your professional and personal spheres are understood and respected.

Initiate an open and honest conversation with your immediate supervisor or manager. Share your joyous news and provide an overview of your upcoming wedding plans. This transparency sets the stage for a collaborative discussion about potential adjustments to your workload or schedule. Approach the conversation with a proactive mindset, seeking solutions that benefit both you and the organization.

When communicating your boundaries, be clear about your expectations and limitations. If you anticipate needing flexibility in your work hours or occasional time off for wedding-related appointments, express this candidly. Clearly defined expectations foster a supportive work environment, enabling your colleagues to understand your needs and contribute to a collaborative atmosphere.

Consider proposing a structured plan for managing your workload during peak wedding planning periods. This could involve strategizing deadlines, redistributing tasks, or temporarily adjusting your role's responsibilities. By presenting a thought-out plan, you demonstrate your commitment to maintaining productivity while navigating the demands of wedding preparations.

Articulate the importance of maintaining a healthy work-life balance. Emphasize that while you are committed to fulfilling your professional responsibilities, you also recognize the significance of investing time and energy into personal milestones. Framing the conversation in terms of balance and well-being fosters understanding and encourages a supportive workplace culture.

Encourage an ongoing dialogue with your colleagues. Make it clear that you are open to discussions about how to collectively ensure that work responsibilities are managed effectively. Establishing a collaborative atmosphere encourages your colleagues to share their needs and boundaries as well, fostering a sense of mutual respect and understanding.

Communicate any temporary changes to your availability promptly. If you anticipate periods where your attention may be more focused on wedding planning, inform your colleagues in advance. This proactive communication allows for adjustments to be made seamlessly, preventing last-minute disruptions and ensuring a smooth workflow.

Educate your colleagues about the significance of your wedding day. While they may understand the logistical aspects of wedding planning, sharing the emotional importance of this milestone helps create empathy and support. Letting them know that you appreciate their understanding and flexibility reinforces the sense of camaraderie within the workplace.

Establish boundaries for communication outside of working hours. In the age of constant connectivity, it's crucial to set clear expectations about when you are available for work-related communication. Establishing dedicated times for professional correspondence ensures that you can fully immerse yourself in wedding planning without feeling tethered to work obligations during personal moments.

If applicable, consider exploring flexible work arrangements. Depending on your job and company policies, options such as remote work, flexible hours, or compressed workweeks could provide additional flexibility during the wedding planning process. Initiate a conversation about these possibilities and work collaboratively to find solutions that align with both your needs and the organization's requirements.

In conclusion, communicating boundaries with employers and colleagues is an integral aspect of successfully balancing work and wedding planning. By approaching these conversations with transparency, proactive solutions, and a commitment to maintaining a healthy work-life balance, you contribute to a supportive work environment that acknowledges and celebrates the multifaceted aspects of your life. As you navigate this communication journey, may it be characterized by understanding, collaboration, and a shared commitment to both your professional and personal success.

Incorporating Short Breaks for Mental Refreshment

In the intricate dance of balancing work and wedding planning, incorporating short breaks for mental refreshment emerges as a secret weapon—an intentional practice that rejuvenates your mind, fosters creativity, and contributes to sustained productivity. These brief respites from the demands of your dual roles serve as essential moments of self-care, ensuring that you navigate both realms with clarity and enthusiasm.

Consider short breaks as a form of mental reset button. In the fast-paced world of work and wedding planning, your mind can become a bustling hub of thoughts, decisions, and to-do lists. Short breaks provide an opportunity to step back, take a breath, and momentarily disengage from the mental whirlwind. Whether it's a stroll around the office, a few minutes of deep breathing, or a gaze out the window, these moments of pause recalibrate your focus and energy.

Integrate micro-moments of mindfulness into your short breaks. Mindful practices, such as brief meditation or focused breathing exercises, become powerful tools for grounding yourself in the present moment. As you navigate the intricacies of both work and wedding planning, these intentional moments of mindfulness foster mental clarity, reduce stress, and contribute to an overall sense of well-being.

Explore the benefits of physical movement during your breaks. Whether it's a quick stretch, a brief walk, or even a few yoga poses, incorporating movement into your short breaks enhances blood circulation, releases tension, and invigorates your body and mind. Physical activity becomes a natural antidote to the sedentary aspects of office work and the mental demands of wedding planning.

Step outside during your breaks to embrace the revitalizing power of nature. A breath of fresh air, a moment in the sunshine, or a brief connection with the natural world contributes to mental refreshment. Even in a bustling urban environment, finding a quiet outdoor spot can provide a welcome respite from the controlled indoor settings of both the workplace and wedding planning spaces.

Embrace the social aspect of short breaks. Engaging in light conversation with colleagues or friends during these moments creates a sense of camaraderie and community. Sharing a laugh, discussing non-work-related topics, or simply enjoying a brief social connection fosters positive relationships and contributes to a supportive environment.

Consider incorporating short breaks as transition periods between work and wedding planning tasks. As you shift from professional responsibilities to wedding-related activities, or vice versa, take a few minutes to consciously transition. This could involve a brief mindfulness exercise, a moment of reflection, or even a symbolic action that signals the shift in focus. Transition breaks allow you to approach each realm with a fresh perspective.

Emphasize the importance of unplugging during your short breaks. In the age of constant connectivity, taking moments to detach from emails, notifications, and the demands of technology becomes crucial. Allow yourself to fully immerse in the present moment without the distractions of electronic devices, fostering a sense of mental clarity and reducing the risk of burnout.

Recognize that short breaks are not indulgences but essential components of a balanced and productive day. In the pursuit of efficiency, it's easy to overlook the value of brief respites. However, these intentional breaks contribute to sustained focus, heightened creativity, and overall well-being. Consider short breaks as investments in your mental and emotional resilience, allowing you to navigate both the world of work and the realm of wedding planning with grace and enthusiasm.

In conclusion, incorporating short breaks for mental refreshment is a powerful practice that transcends the boundaries of work and wedding planning. By weaving these moments of pause into your daily routine, you not only enhance your productivity but also nurture your well-being. May these brief respites become cherished opportunities for rejuvenation, reflection, and a touch of joy as you navigate the intricate dance of balancing both worlds.

Chapter 11: Cultivating Gratitude

Welcome to Chapter 11: Cultivating Gratitude—a chapter that invites you to embark on a transformative journey of appreciation and mindfulness. In the midst of the excitement and intricacies of wedding planning, cultivating gratitude emerges as a powerful practice, offering a lens through which to view both the challenges and joys of this significant chapter in your life.

Gratitude, in its essence, is the art of acknowledging and appreciating the blessings that surround us. As a working bride navigating the landscape of professional responsibilities and wedding preparations, the practice of gratitude becomes a beacon of positivity—a way to navigate the sometimes overwhelming sea of details with a heart full of appreciation.

In this chapter, we'll explore the multifaceted benefits of incorporating gratitude into your daily life. Beyond being a fleeting emotion, gratitude becomes a conscious and intentional practice that has the potential to shape your perspective, enhance your well-being, and infuse your wedding journey with a sense of joy and fulfillment.

As you embark on the adventure of planning one of the most significant days of your life, cultivating gratitude becomes a grounding force. It allows you to appreciate the journey as much as the destination, finding moments of joy in the small details, and recognizing the support and love that surrounds you.

Together, we'll explore practical ways to infuse gratitude into your daily routine. From expressing appreciation for the people who contribute to your wedding preparations to finding moments of reflection and thankfulness amidst the busyness, the journey of cultivating gratitude is as unique as your wedding vision.

Gratitude becomes a guiding light, offering solace during moments of stress, a perspective shift during challenges, and a source of joy during the celebrations. So, as you turn the pages of this chapter, let gratitude be your companion—a gentle reminder to pause, appreciate, and savor the richness of the journey you're on. May this practice become a cherished part of your wedding preparations, transforming not only the way you approach planning but also the way you experience the profound moments that lead you to the altar.

The Power of Gratitude in Wedding Planning

In the whirlwind of wedding planning, where decisions abound, timelines loom, and to-do lists seem endless, the power of gratitude emerges as a transformative force—a quiet yet profound ally that shapes your perspective and infuses your journey with positivity.

At its core, gratitude is not just a fleeting emotion but a conscious practice of recognizing and appreciating the abundance that surrounds you. As a working bride, navigating the intricate dance of professional commitments and wedding preparations, integrating gratitude into this process becomes a beacon of light that illuminates the joy woven into each moment.

One of the remarkable aspects of gratitude is its ability to shift your focus from what might be perceived as lacking to the abundance that already exists. In the context of wedding planning, this means acknowledging the support, love, and resources that contribute to making your dream day a reality. By fostering an attitude of gratitude, you cultivate resilience in the face of challenges and elevate the entire planning experience.

Consider the influence of gratitude on your relationships. As you embark on this shared journey with your partner, family, and friends, expressing gratitude becomes a profound way to strengthen bonds. Acknowledge the time, effort, and love that others invest in your wedding, recognizing that their contributions, whether big or small, are essential threads in the tapestry of your celebration.

Gratitude also serves as a powerful antidote to stress. When faced with the myriad details of wedding planning, moments of overwhelm may arise. However, pausing to reflect on the positive aspects—whether it's the support of your wedding team, the excitement of envisioning your special day, or the joyous anticipation of the celebration—can ground you in a space of appreciation, alleviating stress and providing clarity.

The practice of gratitude extends beyond external factors to your own inner experience. Acknowledge the personal growth, resilience, and creativity that emerge during this process. Celebrate the moments of joy, the lessons learned, and the discovery of your own strengths. Gratitude becomes a mirror that reflects not only the external blessings but also the richness of your own journey.

Expressing gratitude is not solely reserved for the culmination of the wedding day; it becomes an integral part of the entire process. From the initial stages of planning to the final celebrations, take moments to pause and express appreciation. Share your gratitude with your partner, express it in conversations with your wedding team, and reflect on it in private moments of contemplation.

As you navigate the intricacies of wedding planning, consider incorporating gratitude into your daily routine. It doesn't require grand gestures; it can be as simple as reflecting on three things you are grateful for each day. This intentional practice creates a positive ripple effect, influencing your mindset, your interactions, and the overall energy surrounding your wedding preparations.

In conclusion, the power of gratitude in wedding planning is transformative. It becomes a guiding force that shapes your perspective, strengthens your relationships, and enhances your overall well-being. As you embark on this journey, allow gratitude to be woven into the fabric of your preparations, creating a tapestry of joy, appreciation, and love. May your wedding planning journey be not just a checklist of tasks but a rich and fulfilling adventure, with gratitude as your ever-present companion.

Keeping a Gratitude Journal

Keeping a gratitude journal is a delightful and introspective practice that can bring a profound shift to your mindset during the wedding planning journey. As a working bride balancing professional commitments and the intricacies of wedding preparations, a gratitude journal becomes a personal sanctuary—a space where you intentionally capture moments of joy, appreciation, and reflection.

The concept of a gratitude journal is beautifully simple. It involves regularly recording things you are grateful for, whether big or small, in a dedicated journal or notebook. This practice transcends the routine tasks of wedding planning, inviting you to weave a tapestry of gratitude that encompasses the broader landscape of your life during this transformative period.

Begin by choosing a journal that resonates with you. It could be a beautifully crafted notebook, a digital journal, or any medium that feels comfortable for you to express your thoughts. The act of choosing a journal becomes the first step in creating a sacred space where you can unfold your inner reflections.

Set a consistent time for your gratitude journaling. Whether it's at the beginning or end of the day, find a moment when you can immerse yourself in this practice without distractions. This regular ritual allows you to cultivate a sense of mindfulness, creating a pause in your day to reflect on the positive aspects of your life.

As you embark on this journey, let your entries be authentic and diverse. Gratitude doesn't solely revolve around major milestones; it thrives in the small, everyday moments. Reflect on the support you receive, the laughter shared with loved ones, the progress made in wedding planning, or even the serenity found in moments of solitude. Your entries become a mosaic that captures the multifaceted beauty of your life.

Use descriptive language to articulate your gratitude. Instead of merely stating what you're grateful for, delve into the details. If you appreciate the support of your partner, describe the specific actions or words that touched your heart. If you find joy in the beauty of wedding details, articulate the colors, textures, or sentiments that evoke appreciation. Adding detail to your entries deepens your connection to the moments you're acknowledging.

Allow your gratitude journal to serve as a refuge during challenging moments. In the midst of wedding planning stress or work-related pressures, turn to your journal as a source of solace. Reading through past entries reminds you of the positivity and joy that coexists with challenges. It becomes a personal archive of resilience and a testament to the abundance in your life.

Consider incorporating reflective prompts into your gratitude journaling. These prompts can guide your thoughts and inspire deeper contemplation. For instance, you might explore what you've learned about yourself during the wedding planning process or express gratitude for unexpected moments of support. Prompts provide a gentle nudge, encouraging you to explore different facets of your experience.

Share your gratitude journey with your partner if you feel inclined. Whether you read entries to each other or discuss moments of appreciation together, sharing this practice becomes a beautiful way to deepen your connection during the wedding planning process. It fosters open communication and strengthens the bond between you as you navigate this significant chapter together.

In conclusion, keeping a gratitude journal during wedding planning is a meaningful and transformative practice. It becomes a cherished companion, offering you a haven of positivity and reflection amid the bustling details of this chapter. As you pen down moments of appreciation, may your gratitude journal be a testimony to the richness of your experience—a tapestry woven with the threads of joy, love, and gratitude.

Expressing Appreciation to Your Support System

Expressing appreciation to your support system is a heartfelt and essential practice that weaves gratitude into the fabric of your wedding planning journey. In the midst of the excitement, decisions, and occasional challenges, acknowledging the contributions of your support system becomes a meaningful way to strengthen connections and infuse your preparations with positivity.

Your support system encompasses a diverse group of individuals—partners, family members, friends, and even colleagues—who play pivotal roles in different aspects of your wedding planning. From emotional support to practical assistance, expressing gratitude to this network of individuals is an opportunity to foster connection and reciprocate the love and energy they invest in your journey.

Begin by reflecting on the unique contributions of each person in your support system. Consider the emotional support provided by your partner, the wisdom shared by family members, the enthusiasm of friends, and the understanding of colleagues. Each role is distinct, and expressing gratitude allows you to honor the diverse ways in which people show up for you.

Choose authentic and personalized ways to express your appreciation. While a heartfelt thank-you is always meaningful, consider tailoring your expressions of gratitude to resonate with the individual's personality and preferences. This could involve a handwritten note, a thoughtful gesture, or even a shared moment that holds significance for both of you. Personalized expressions of gratitude carry a special resonance that reflects the depth of your connection.

Don't underestimate the power of specific and detailed appreciation. Instead of generic expressions of thanks, delve into the specifics of what you appreciate about each person. Acknowledge the unique qualities, actions, or support that have made a tangible impact on your wedding planning experience. Specificity enhances the sincerity of your gratitude and communicates that you've genuinely noticed and valued their contributions.

Consider creating personalized moments of appreciation. Whether it's a small gathering, a surprise gesture, or a heartfelt conversation, providing intentional moments of gratitude adds a layer of significance to your expressions. Create an environment that allows you to openly express your thanks, share reflections on the journey, and celebrate the collaborative spirit that defines your support system.

Embrace the power of surprise. While expressing gratitude during major milestones is expected, consider incorporating moments of surprise appreciation. It could be a spontaneous note, a surprise thank-you event, or even a heartfelt message during a casual conversation. Surprise expressions of gratitude carry an element of spontaneity that heightens their impact.

Expressing gratitude is not limited to words; actions can speak volumes. Show your appreciation through supportive gestures, thoughtful actions, or by actively participating in shared responsibilities. Actions that align with your words reinforce the authenticity of your gratitude and contribute to a reciprocal dynamic within your support system.

Celebrate your support system collectively. Consider organizing a gathering, dinner, or event where you can collectively express your gratitude. This shared celebration becomes an opportunity not only to express thanks but also to foster a sense of community and connection among the individuals supporting you. It reinforces the notion that your wedding planning journey is a collaborative effort.

Remember that expressing gratitude is an ongoing practice. While major milestones provide natural opportunities for appreciation, consider incorporating gratitude into your everyday interactions. Regular expressions of thanks, whether big or small, contribute to a positive and supportive atmosphere that extends beyond the specific context of wedding planning.

In conclusion, expressing appreciation to your support system is a beautiful and reciprocal practice that elevates the energy of your wedding planning journey. As you navigate this significant chapter, let gratitude be the thread that weaves through your connections, creating a tapestry of love, support, and celebration. May your expressions of thanks contribute to the joy and harmony that define your relationships, making your wedding preparations not only a shared endeavor but also a collective celebration of the bonds that enrich your life.

Chapter 12: Post-Wedding Self-Care

Welcome to Chapter 12: Post-Wedding Self-Care—a chapter that extends the journey of self-care beyond the celebration and into the phase that follows the exchange of vows. As the echoes of your wedding day linger in your heart and the joyous memories settle, this chapter becomes a guide to nurturing yourself in the aftermath of this momentous event.

Post-wedding self-care is a gentle reminder that the journey doesn't end at the altar; it evolves into a new chapter filled with reflection, adjustment, and the beginning of shared dreams. In the midst of transitioning from the whirlwind of wedding planning to the rhythm of married life, taking intentional moments for self-care becomes not only a luxury but a necessity.

In these pages, we'll explore the art of navigating the post-wedding phase with grace and mindfulness. From emotional well-being to the practical aspects of settling into married life, this chapter is designed to be a companion—a source of support as you transition from the heightened emotions of the wedding day to the everyday beauty of shared moments and quiet joy.

The post-wedding phase often comes with a mix of emotions. There's the bliss of being newlyweds, the nostalgia for the vibrant celebrations, and the potential for a gentle adjustment to the rhythm of life after the wedding. This chapter is here to provide guidance on caring for yourself during this multifaceted period, ensuring that you embark on the journey of marriage with a sense of balance and well-being.

As you turn the pages, consider this a space to reflect on the beautiful tapestry of your wedding day and to navigate the exciting, sometimes unpredictable, terrain that follows. Post-wedding self-care is a way to honor the love that brought you to this moment and to nurture the connection that will carry you forward. May this chapter be a source of inspiration and practical insights, guiding you toward a post-wedding phase filled with self-discovery, shared joy, and the warm embrace of the love you've celebrated and vowed to cherish.

Transitioning to Married Life: What to Expect

Embarking on the journey of married life is a beautiful transition, and much like any significant change, it comes with its own set of adjustments and discoveries. In this section, we'll explore what to expect as you transition from the excitement of wedding celebrations to the everyday magic of being a married couple.

Firstly, it's essential to acknowledge that the post-wedding period is a time of adjustment. The heightened emotions of the wedding day may start to settle, and you'll find yourself navigating the rhythm of daily life as a married couple. This doesn't mean the end of excitement but rather the beginning of a different kind of joy—a joy that is woven into the ordinary moments of shared breakfasts, quiet evenings, and the comfort of being together.

Communication plays a pivotal role in this transition. As you step into married life, there's a beautiful opportunity to deepen your connection through open and honest communication. Share your thoughts, dreams, and even any concerns you might have. This is a time to cultivate a sense of shared vision for your life together, understanding each other's expectations and aspirations.

Expect a blend of routines and new experiences. Married life often involves a harmonious mix of established routines and the excitement of creating new traditions together. Embrace the comfort of familiar rituals while exploring new adventures that define your unique journey as a couple. Whether it's cooking together, planning weekend getaways, or simply enjoying quiet evenings, finding the balance between the known and the novel is part of the charm.

There might be moments of nostalgia for the wedding day, and that's perfectly natural. The vibrancy of the celebrations, the love of friends and family, and the joyous atmosphere are memories that will hold a special place in your heart. Allow yourself to revisit those memories, perhaps through photographs or shared stories, but also relish in the present moment of being together in your newlywed bliss.

Navigating shared responsibilities is an integral aspect of transitioning to married life. From household chores to financial decisions, finding a rhythm that feels equitable and supportive is key. This is a collaborative journey where you both contribute to the tapestry of your shared life. Embrace teamwork, communication, and a sense of shared responsibility as you build the foundation for a fulfilling married life.

The post-wedding period is also an opportunity for individual growth within the context of your partnership. As you navigate this transition, you may discover new facets of yourselves and each other. Embrace the beauty of continuous self-discovery and encourage each other's personal and professional growth.

Finally, remember that there is no one-size-fits-all roadmap for transitioning to married life. Every couple's journey is unique, shaped by your personalities, values, and shared dreams. Allow yourselves the grace to grow and evolve together, savoring the unfolding chapters of your love story.

In conclusion, transitioning to married life is a beautiful and dynamic process. It's a time of adjustment, communication, shared responsibilities, and the creation of a shared life that reflects the unique essence of your love. As you step into this new chapter, may it be filled with the warmth of shared moments, the joy of building a life together, and the enduring love that brought you to this beautiful milestone.

Reflecting on the Wedding Journey

Reflecting on the wedding journey is a poignant and introspective practice that allows you to revisit the milestones, emotions, and growth experienced during the process of planning and celebrating your union. As you settle into married life, taking time to reflect on the wedding journey becomes a meaningful way to honor the richness of this transformative period.

Begin by acknowledging the diverse range of emotions that characterized your wedding journey. From the initial stages of excitement and anticipation to the moments of stress and decision-making, each emotion has played a vital role in shaping your experience. Reflecting on this emotional spectrum allows you to appreciate the depth of your journey and the resilience you've demonstrated in navigating various challenges.

Consider revisiting the memories of your wedding day. Whether through photographs, videos, or shared stories, immerse yourself in the joy, laughter, and love that defined that special day. Reflect on the meaningful moments—the exchange of vows, the shared glances, and the dance floor celebrations. These memories serve as cherished treasures that continue to radiate warmth as you transition into the post-wedding phase.

Reflecting on the wedding journey also involves acknowledging the growth and learning that occurred along the way. Wedding planning is a unique experience that often involves discovering new facets of yourself and your partner. Consider the skills you've developed, the challenges you've overcome, and the teamwork that defined your preparations. This introspection becomes a foundation for continuous personal and relational growth in the context of your marriage.

Take a moment to express gratitude for the individuals who contributed to your wedding journey. From family and friends to the wedding team who brought your vision to life, expressing appreciation fosters a sense of connection and reinforces the bonds that were strengthened during this period. Gratitude becomes a bridge that connects the wedding journey to the ongoing tapestry of your relationships.

Consider creating a tangible representation of your wedding journey—a scrapbook, a journal, or even a piece of art that encapsulates the essence of your experience. This creative endeavor becomes a keepsake that you can revisit in the years to come, a tangible reminder of the love, support, and joy that surrounded your wedding.

Reflecting on the wedding journey is also an opportunity to set intentions for the future. As you navigate the post-wedding phase, consider the values, dreams, and shared goals that will shape your life together. This forward-looking reflection becomes a roadmap for the adventures and milestones that lie ahead, infusing your marriage with purpose and shared vision.

Remember that reflection is a personal and ongoing practice. It doesn't require grand gestures; it can be as simple as a quiet moment of contemplation or a shared conversation with your partner. The beauty of reflection lies in its ability to deepen your connection to the journey you've undertaken and to nurture the love that brought you to this beautiful chapter of married life.

In conclusion, reflecting on the wedding journey is a tender and profound practice that allows you to honor the past, appreciate the present, and set intentions for the future. As you turn the pages of this reflective chapter, may it be a time of gratitude, introspection, and the celebration of the enduring love that weaves through the threads of your wedding journey.

Continuing Self-Care Practices Beyond the Big Day

Continuing self-care practices beyond the big day is a thoughtful and intentional investment in the well-being of your relationship and individual fulfillment. As the echoes of wedding celebrations linger and you settle into the rhythm of married life, integrating self-care into your routine becomes a sustaining force that nurtures the love that brought you together.

One of the key aspects of post-wedding self-care is maintaining the positive habits and routines cultivated during the wedding planning phase. Whether it's mindfulness practices, regular exercise, or moments of quiet reflection, these habits contribute to your overall well-being and can serve as anchors amid the ebb and flow of everyday life. Consistency in self-care fosters a sense of balance and resilience, enhancing your ability to navigate challenges with a grounded and centered mindset.

Communication continues to be a cornerstone of self-care in marriage. Keep the lines of communication open with your partner, expressing your needs, desires, and concerns. Share your reflections on the wedding journey and discuss how you envision incorporating self-care into your shared life. Mutual understanding and support create a nurturing environment where both partners feel valued and heard.

Explore new self-care practices that align with your evolving life as a couple. As you settle into the routines of married life, consider activities that bring you joy, relaxation, and a sense of connection. This could involve shared hobbies, weekend getaways, or even simple rituals like cooking together or enjoying a quiet evening stroll. The beauty of continuing self-care practices is that they can be tailored to the unique dynamics of your relationship.

Celebrate milestones, both big and small, as opportunities for self-care and shared joy. Whether it's commemorating anniversaries, achieving personal or professional goals, or simply relishing the joy of everyday moments, marking these occasions becomes a way to acknowledge and celebrate the journey you're on together. These celebrations contribute to a positive and appreciative mindset, enhancing the overall well-being of your marriage.

Consider integrating moments of solitude into your routine. While shared experiences are integral to a thriving marriage, individual moments of self-reflection and rejuvenation are equally important. Whether it's reading a book, pursuing a personal hobby, or enjoying a quiet cup of tea, allowing space for individual self-care contributes to a holistic and balanced approach to well-being.

Self-care also involves adapting to the changing seasons of life. As your journey as a married couple unfolds, priorities may shift, and new responsibilities may emerge. Embrace the flexibility to adjust your self-care practices accordingly. This adaptability ensures that your self-care routine remains dynamic, responsive to the evolving needs of both individuals and the relationship.

Lastly, cherish the love and connection that brought you to this point. Actively nurture the emotional bond that defines your marriage through expressions of affection, shared laughter, and moments of vulnerability. Building a foundation of emotional intimacy is a form of self-care that contributes to the overall health and resilience of your relationship.

In conclusion, continuing self-care practices beyond the big day is a deliberate and ongoing commitment to the well-being of your marriage. As you navigate the post-wedding phase, may self-care become an integral thread woven into the fabric of your shared life. Whether through established routines, open communication, shared celebrations, or moments of solitude, let self-care be a source of nourishment that enhances the depth, joy, and enduring love that characterize your journey as a married couple.

Conclusion: Embracing a Radiant Future

As we reach the conclusion of this journey together, it's a moment to reflect on the tapestry of self-care woven into the fabric of wedding planning and the transition into married life. "Embracing a Radiant Future" is not just a conclusion; it's an invitation to envision the beautiful chapters that await you as a couple. Through the highs and lows, the celebrations and quiet moments, this conclusion serves as a guidepost, beckoning you toward a future filled with love, connection, and well-being.

The beauty of this moment lies in the recognition that your wedding day is not the culmination but the commencement of a radiant future. The practices of self-care, reflection, and intentional living that you've cultivated along this journey are seeds planted for the flourishing garden of your marriage. As you stand at the threshold of what comes next, know that the pages of your love story are still being written, and each chapter is an opportunity to infuse your shared narrative with joy, resilience, and the warmth of a love that evolves and deepens over time.

"Embracing a Radiant Future" is an ode to the possibilities that unfold when a couple consciously tends to the well-being of their relationship. It's an acknowledgment that marriage is not a destination but a continuous journey—a journey that thrives when nurtured with care, communication, and shared moments of joy. This conclusion invites you to carry forward the spirit of self-care, not as a fleeting practice but as a steadfast companion, guiding you through the complexities and celebrations that await.

As you turn the last pages of this book, consider it a prelude to the unwritten chapters of your marriage. The future is radiant, not because it promises perfection, but because it holds the potential for growth, discovery, and the shared joy that comes from navigating life together. May your future be adorned with the glow of love, the strength of connection, and the enduring beauty of a journey well-lived. The curtain falls on this book, but the stage is set for the radiant performance of your marriage, where every day is an opportunity to embrace the brilliance of a shared and ever-evolving future.

Summarizing Key Self-Care Principles

As we bring this insightful journey to a close, it's time to distill the essence of the key self-care principles that have been woven into the fabric of this book. These principles are not just guidelines for the duration of wedding planning—they are enduring truths that extend into the beautiful expanse of married life. Let's take a moment to reflect on these principles, recognizing them as the pillars upon which the foundation of a resilient, joyous, and fulfilling marriage can be built.

1. Prioritizing Well-Being: At the heart of self-care lies the commitment to prioritize your well-being. Whether it's during the whirlwind of wedding preparations or the everyday routine of married life, recognizing the importance of self-care is an affirmation that your mental, emotional, and physical health are foundational to the strength of your relationship.

2. Mindful Communication: Communication is the lifeblood of any relationship, and it becomes even more vital during the intense period of wedding planning. The principle of mindful communication emphasizes the significance of expressing needs, actively listening, and fostering an environment where open and honest dialogue can flourish. This principle extends into the post-wedding phase, becoming a cornerstone for the continued growth of your connection.

3. Embracing Flexibility: The journey of wedding planning is a dynamic one, filled with unexpected twists and turns. Embracing flexibility is a guiding principle that encourages adaptability in the face of challenges. This flexibility extends into married life, acknowledging that the ability to pivot and adjust is a valuable asset in navigating the ever-changing landscape of a shared life.

4. Nurturing Emotional Intimacy: Emotional intimacy is the heartbeat of a thriving marriage. The self-care principle of nurturing emotional intimacy involves cultivating a deep and meaningful connection with your partner. Whether through shared vulnerabilities,

expressions of love, or moments of shared joy, emotional intimacy becomes a source of strength that sustains the warmth and closeness in your relationship.

5. Celebrating Individuality: Self-care isn't just about collective well-being; it's also about honoring and celebrating individuality. Recognizing and supporting each other's unique identities, aspirations, and growth is a self-care principle that contributes to the holistic health of your marriage. It's an acknowledgment that a strong partnership is built on the foundation of two individuals thriving together.

6. Continuous Reflection: The practice of continuous reflection is a self-care principle that extends beyond the wedding day. It involves regularly pausing to examine the journey, acknowledge growth, and set intentions for the future. This reflective approach becomes a compass, guiding you through the various seasons of your marriage with mindfulness and purpose.

7. Integrating Joy into Everyday Moments: Self-care isn't reserved for special occasions; it's a principle that encourages the infusion of joy into the tapestry of everyday moments. Whether it's a shared meal, a quiet evening, or a spontaneous adventure, the intentional integration of joy becomes a source of sustenance that elevates the ordinary into the extraordinary.

As we bid farewell to the pages of this book, may these self-care principles serve as beacons of light, illuminating the path toward a radiant future. Your marriage is an unfolding story, and these principles are the narrative threads that weave through the chapters, creating a tapestry of love, connection, and well-being. Embrace these principles not as mandates but as invitations—to care for yourself, nurture your relationship, and embark on the boundless journey of a love that grows more radiant with each passing day.